IMISCOE Research Series

This series is the official book series of IMISCOE, the largest network of excellence on migration and diversity in the world. It comprises publications which present empirical and theoretical research on different aspects of international migration. The authors are all specialists, and the publications a rich source of information for researchers and others involved in international migration studies. The series is published under the editorial supervision of the IMISCOE Editorial Committee which includes leading scholars from all over Europe. The series, which contains more than eighty titles already, is internationally peer reviewed which ensures that the book published in this series continue to present excellent academic standards and scholarly quality. Most of the books are available open access.

Magdalena Nordin • Jonas Otterbeck

Migration and Religion

IMISCOE Short Reader

 Springer

Magdalena Nordin
University of Gothenburg
Gothenburg, Sweden

Jonas Otterbeck
Institute for the Study of Muslim Civilisations
Aga Khan University
London, UK

ISSN 2364-4087   ISSN 2364-4095 (electronic)
IMISCOE Research Series
ISBN 978-3-031-30765-2   ISBN 978-3-031-30766-9 (eBook)
https://doi.org/10.1007/978-3-031-30766-9

This work was supported by IMISCOE

© The Editor(s) (if applicable) and The Author(s) 2023. This book is an open access publication.

Open Access This book is licensed under the terms of the Creative Commons Attribution 4.0 International License (http://creativecommons.org/licenses/by/4.0/), which permits use, sharing, adaptation, distribution and reproduction in any medium or format, as long as you give appropriate credit to the original author(s) and the source, provide a link to the Creative Commons license and indicate if changes were made.

The images or other third party material in this book are included in the book's Creative Commons license, unless indicated otherwise in a credit line to the material. If material is not included in the book's Creative Commons license and your intended use is not permitted by statutory regulation or exceeds the permitted use, you will need to obtain permission directly from the copyright holder.

The use of general descriptive names, registered names, trademarks, service marks, etc. in this publication does not imply, even in the absence of a specific statement, that such names are exempt from the relevant protective laws and regulations and therefore free for general use.

The publisher, the authors, and the editors are safe to assume that the advice and information in this book are believed to be true and accurate at the date of publication. Neither the publisher nor the authors or the editors give a warranty, expressed or implied, with respect to the material contained herein or for any errors or omissions that may have been made. The publisher remains neutral with regard to jurisdictional claims in published maps and institutional affiliations.

This Springer imprint is published by the registered company Springer Nature Switzerland AG
The registered company address is: Gewerbestrasse 11, 6330 Cham, Switzerland

Preface

This book is the outcome of years of discussions between the two authors while colleagues at Lund and Malmö Universities, both in Sweden. It is also the result of years of research and teaching on related subjects. Both of us have specialised in migration studies and religious studies – Magdalena Nordin from the perspective of sociology of religion and Jonas Otterbeck from Islamic studies. Since 2017, Nordin has been associate professor at the Department of Literature, History of Ideas and Religion at Gothenburg University, and in 2018, Otterbeck was appointed professor at the Aga Khan University – Institute for the Study of Muslim Civilisations, London.

We would like to acknowledge the economic support of Birgit and Sven Håkan Ohlsson's Foundation and the Berndt Gustafsson's memorial fund for the sociology of church and religion in producing this book. We would also like to extend thanks to Professors Garbi Schmidt and Tuomas Martikainen who gave us some fine ideas at a panel the four of us arranged for the annual IMISCOE conference at Malmö University in 2019. Finally, we would like to acknowledge the importance of the support we have received from the Centre for Theology and Religious Studies at Lund University, the Aga Khan University – Institute for the Study of Muslim Civilisations, the Department of Literature, History of Ideas and Religion at Gothenburg University and IMISCOE.

This book is dedicated to all students, colleagues, interviewees, friends and family who have shared their stories of migration with us, experiences that are real and important. After all, many have been international migrants at some stage in their lives, as have both of us.

Gothenburg, Sweden   Magdalena Nordin

London, UK   Jonas Otterbeck

Contents

Part I Researching Migration and Religion

1 Introducing the Field: 'Migration and Religion' 3
   1.1 Constant Migrations... 3
   1.2 The Aim of This Book...................................... 4
   1.3 Migrants and Migration 5
   1.4 Religion 6
        1.4.1 Religion and Secularisation in Europe................. 7
   1.5 Religion and Migration 9
   1.6 The Complicated Task of Finding Things Out................. 10
   1.7 Religion, Migration and Integration 13
   1.8 Religion and Migration from an Intersectional Perspective 14
   References.. 15

2 Trends in Research: A Literature Review....................... 19
   2.1 Early Research (1903–1970s) 19
        2.1.1 Summary 22
   2.2 Scholarship in the 1980s and 1990s.......................... 23
        2.2.1 American Scholarship 23
        2.2.2 European Scholarship 26
   2.3 European Scholarship from 2000–2010....................... 28
   2.4 European and Some American Scholarship from 2010.......... 30
   2.5 Concluding Remarks 31
   References.. 32

Part II The New Home

**3   Finding Tactics and Making Space: The Individuals
     and the Communities** 43
     3.1   The Social Functions of Religion 44
           3.1.1   Demographics 44
           3.1.2   Religion as a Social Structure 44
           3.1.3   Morals and the Bracketing of Them 45
           3.1.4   Gender, Social Norms, and Integration 46
     3.2   The Migrant's Religious Life and Its Effects................. 47
           3.2.1   Ritualisation and Quotidian Rituals................... 48
           3.2.2   Ritualisation and Lifecycle Rituals 49
           3.2.3   Religion as a Resource or Hindrance for Integration...... 50
           3.2.4   Religion and Active Citizenship 52
     3.3   The Establishment of Religious Organisations 53
           3.3.1   The Patterns of Establishment 53
           3.3.2   The Processes of Space Making
                   and the Emotions Involved.......................... 55
           3.3.3   Support and Conflict 56
     3.4   Transnational Spaces and Global Movements................. 57
           3.4.1   Transnational Spaces and Social Remittances........... 58
           3.4.2   Global Religious Movements........................ 60
     3.5   Religious Services: A Crossroad of Individual
           and Community Tactics and Space Making.................. 61
           3.5.1   Black Christian Communities in the UK
                   and Congregational Services 62
           3.5.2   Language Groups Within Migrant Communities
                   in Sweden... 62
           3.5.3   Religious Services in Tamil Hindu Temples
                   in Switzerland 63
     3.6   Concluding Remarks 64
     References.. 64

**4   Negotiating Space: Strategies of the European States
     and Politics of Religion**...................................... 69
     4.1   Politics of Religion in History and Today 71
           4.1.1   The Westphalian Settlement......................... 71
           4.1.2   The Neighbourhood, the State, or the Transnational?..... 72
           4.1.3   Governances of Religion(s) 73
     4.2   Rights, Obligations and Laws 74
           4.2.1   Acknowledging Religious Group Rights............... 75
           4.2.2   Freedom of Religion 76
           4.2.3   Blasphemy and Anti-discrimination Laws.............. 76

	4.3	Getting to Know Each Other and Areas of Conflicts............	77
		4.3.1 Religion in Public Institutions......................	78
		4.3.2 Conflict Areas and (Desired) Social Cohesion..........	80
	4.4	Concluding Remarks......................................	83
	References...		84

Part III   Religious Matters

5   Religious Reactions... 89
    5.1   Religious Practices.. 89
           5.1.1   Religious Practices, Generation, and Gender 91
           5.1.2   Perceiving Religious Practices,
                    but Reimagining Them............................. 92
           5.1.3   Abandoning Religious Practices 92
    5.2   Missionaries... 93
           5.2.1   Spreading the Word 93
           5.2.2   Revitalizing Faith................................ 94
           5.2.3   Pastoral Care 95
    5.3   Conversions 96
           5.3.1   What Conversion Can Tell Us About Migration 96
           5.3.2   Conversion and Identity............................ 98
    5.4   New Theologies.. 99
           5.4.1   Liberal Theologies................................ 99
           5.4.2   Revivalist Theologies.............................. 100
           5.4.3   Conservative Theologies 101
           5.4.4   Theologies of Migration 102
    5.5   Charity.. 103
           5.5.1   Migrants' NGO Religious Charities 103
           5.5.2   The Importance of Economic Remittances 104
    5.6   Creativity in the Arts 105
           5.6.1   Art Critical of Religious Expressions
                    in Former Homelands 106
           5.6.2   Art that Is Nostalgic or Celebratory
                    in Relation to Religious Arts in Former Homelands 107
           5.6.3   Arts that Use Popular Art Expressions
                    in the New Homelands to Affirm Religion 107
           5.6.4   Arts for Dialogue................................. 108
    References... 108

6   Looking Ahead 113
    6.1   Bringing Religion into Migration Research.................... 113
           6.1.1   Religion in the Research Design
                    of International Migration 113
           6.1.2   The Function and Spaces of Religion 114
           6.1.3   Changing Religious Norms and Actual Practices 115

6.2	What We Do Not Know		116
	6.2.1	Historical Perspectives	116
	6.2.2	Developing More Reliable Statistics	117
	6.2.3	Comparative Perspectives	118
	6.2.4	The Role of Social Media for Religion in Relation to Migration	118
	6.2.5	Lingering Immigrant Identities	119
	6.2.6	Religious Change in Society in General and Among Established Religious Communities	120
6.3	Final Words		121
References			121

About the Authors

Magdalena Nordin is Associate Professor in Sociology of Religion at the Department of Literature, History of Ideas, and Religion, Gothenburg University, Sweden. Her research has during the last decades been about religion and migration focusing on change of religiosity among migrants, religious plurality and public institutions (such as the healthcare sector and educational institutions), interfaith dialogue, and change, continuity and re-interpretation of religious practices. She is heading the research project "Integration and Tradition: The Making of the Syriac Orthodox Church in Sweden". Among her publications we find "How to Understand Interreligious Dialogue in Sweden in Relation to the Socio-Cultural Context", in the *Interdisciplinary Journal for Religion and Transformation in Contemporary* (2020) and "Rooms of Silence at three universities in Scandinavia", in *Sociology of Religion*: A Quarterly Review (2019).

Jonas Otterbeck is Professor of Islamic Studies at Aga Khan University – Institute for the Study of Muslim Civilisations, London, where he holds the Rasul-Walker Chair in Popular Culture in Islam. His research on Muslims in contemporary Europe spans three decades and topic like Islamic discourse, integration, Muslim youth, conversion, masculinity, popular culture, active citizenship, politics and Islamophobia. Otterbeck's latest monograph is *The Awakening of Islamic Pop Music* (2021, Edinburgh UP). He has published numerous articles and books on Muslim in Europe together with migration researchers like Professors Pieter Bevelander, Garbi Schmidt and Jørgen Nielsen. Otterbeck is on the advisory board of Malmö Institute for Studies of Migration, Diversity and Welfare, Malmö University.

Part I
Researching Migration and Religion

There are people in the world, I imagine, who are born and die in the same town, maybe even in the same house, or bed. Creatures without migration: have they not lived a life because they have not moved?
Novelist Rigoberto González
Butterfly Boy: Memories of a Chicano Mariposa (2006: 168)

Rigoberto Gonazález's *Butterfly Boy* is a personal, heartfelt, coming-of-age – and coming out as gay – narrative set among poor migrants from Mexico who have arrived and settled in the USA. The idea of 'creatures without migration' struck us as a forceful image formulated from a migrant's perspective. Once the move is initiated, will things ever be the same? Not being able, allowed or willing to move becomes deeply problematic, as does the strange category of home. Is it here, there or everywhere? Most importantly, 'creatures without migration' changes perspectives, puts migrants at the centre and prompts the emergence of new questions.

This book introduces research on migration and religion, with a focus on migration to western European countries from the 1950s onwards. It puts together an in-depth presentation of the main research trends in methods, theories and empirical zones connected with migration and religion, assembling research on the topic and aligning it with the experiences and urgencies of migrants. As its aim is to inspire and intrigue, we do not only take established research and theories into account, but also promote new perspectives and challenge some common assumptions in research about migration. We strive to make the reader aware that while the voices of migrants often feature in research, their questions, concerns, resources and religious needs, visions and worldviews are far too often subservient to questions that formulate the concerns of the established majorities. As such, our book is part of a wider trend to re-humanise immigrants. The terminology is drastic, yet speaks volumes about how strange political conversations about migration have become. Luckily, research is generally more sensitive.

Nonetheless, while religious traditions, concerns, rituals and identities are far from ignored in European migration research, they are rarely fully considered.

Researcher engagement is often structured by years of social science research and education that has ignored the theorisation associated with religions. More recent generations of European researchers are better prepared, however, as the complexities surrounding religions are increasingly being included in social science investigations, and, although there is still a great deal to do, much has been done within the field of religion and migration that we will utilise here.

In scholarly terms, we belong to the traditions that study religion as a social phenomenon and as a feature of people's lives. Our motive is not to understand divine sets of ideas better or to learn from religious traditions how to improve the ethics and morals of individuals or groups, although we fully acknowledge the potential importance of such endeavours to people's lives. In fact, that is part of what we study.

The book has three parts and six chapters. The first part – Researching Migration and Religion – introduces key concepts (Chap. 1) and presents a thorough literature review of migration and religion literature, research to which we are both in debt (Chap. 2). Parts II and III aim to provide our perspectives on the complexities surrounding migration and religion. The second part –The New Home – deals with the processes of establishment, on individual and group levels (Chap. 3) as well as on a society level (Chap. 4). The third and final part – Religious Matters – focuses on questions more commonly touched upon in religious studies: religious acts, roles and ideas (Chap. 5). It finishes with a discussion of challenges to research and gaps in our knowledge calling for further investigation (Chap. 6). Parts II and III both aim to stress migration and religion from the migrants' perspective. Thus, the book is a religious studies intervention in migration studies.

Reference

González, R. (2006). *Butterfly boy: Memories of a Chicano mariposa*. Wisconsin: University of Wisconsin Press.

Chapter 1
Introducing the Field: 'Migration and Religion'

In this chapter, we introduce the topic, discuss the aim, define a few key concepts and examine some of the methodological difficulties in researching migration and religion. The chapter aims to make the reader aware of the difference between research and serving up an opinion. Across Europe there are many vocal, opiniated debaters who all too often offer simple answers and quick fixes to identified problems. The very idea behind research is precisely the opposite; it is about grounding rich descriptions and theorisation in carefully crafted, methodologically sound, hard work.

1.1 Constant Migrations

People have always lived lives between being settled and being on the move, either looking for greener pastures, resources to conquer, adventures and new audiences or markets, or trying to get away from whatever unpleasantries they need to avoid: wars, parents, cruel people in power positions, poverty, natural disasters. Often, motives have been mixed. People have explored, clashing and merging with those already in the area just found. Migrants brought with them ideas about the world.

It is impossible to know for certain whether people had organised religious ideas before the invention of writing, coinciding with the first empires of which we are aware, over 5000 years ago. Yet we can craft theories with the help of graves, cave paintings and the remains of prehistoric cities and monuments (e.g., Insoll, 2020), and these indicate that it is highly likely that people have at least nurtured ideas and assumptions about unseen, transcendent and hidden arrangements and logics of the cosmos and the everyday for tens of thousands of years.

When people have met, their respective religious beliefs have fascinated, shocked, instilled hatred and contempt and converted people; as they have come into contact, ideas have mixed and inspired new thought systems. Religious myths and key notions have been exchanged when people have met at royal courts and in taverns; they have been shared between neighbours, lovers and certainly religious specialists of different traditions. We know from history not only of neighbouring traditions meeting, but also, for example, of Greeks practicing their faiths while living in Afghanistan in the many cities founded or conquered by Alexander the Great (d. 323).

Religious ideas move in mysterious ways. For example, the world's numerically largest religion today, Christianity, was carried to Europe in letters, by migrating missionaries and in stories told in marketplaces and at inns. At different times those discussing it were non-Christians, slandering Christianity, wondering over it, asking each other about the truth of what they had heard; many knew about its ideas long before accepting it. Today, ideas move quickly and globally, through social and mass media. Filmed lectures and information pages on religion contain self-presentations as well as criticism and hate speech. Even very small faith groups like the Druze or Zoroastrians are present, but so are new religious movements and sects, like Happy Science, the Japanese movement founded in 1986 and now creating global networks.

1.2 The Aim of This Book

This book is *not* about this rich global history of mobility, meetings and clashes. Rather, the aim is to provide students and researchers with an original account of relevant perspectives, examples and reflections related to religion and to migration to western Europe after WWII. Thus, it is about a mere fragment of history, although one important to societies all over the globe. During the political turmoil in Europe leading up to the war, many Europeans fled their homes for other European countries or destinations such as Australia and North or South America. However, soon the migration tides turned. One may divide migration after WWII into five major trends (inspired by Stalker, 2002): mass refugee flows (1940s and early 1950s); recruitment of contract workers (early 1950s to 1973); restrictive politics (1974 to mid-1980s); diverse migration flows (mid-1980s until 2001); diverse migration flows plus increased securitisation and restriction attempts (2001-ongoing).

By narrowing our focus to western Europe, we consciously exclude most international migrants of the last decades. As a rule, most refugees end up in neighbouring countries and it is a fact that the largest proportion today reside in the so-called Global South. For example, Pakistan is the home to some two to three million Afghans (a figure that was three times as high in the 1990s). Around a million undocumented Bangladeshis and tens of thousands Rohingya also live in Pakistan (Alimia, 2019). The situation is similar in Bangladesh, India and many other countries. However, research on migration in the Global South is a rather new field and in-depth studies analysing religion and migration are few. To date, most theories about religion and migration have been developed in relation to Europe and North America, and as the aim of this book is to introduce theorisation and perspectives on religion and migration – and as the scope must be limited – we have chosen western

Europe as our focus. However, we hope that our writing can also inspire researchers looking into migration in the Global South to expand this field.

The observant reader will have noted the lower case 'western', used to indicate the geographical area of western Europe, not the political and now outdated concept of Western Europe. Yet the migration history of western Europe is different from that of eastern Europe (and that of the southern most parts).

Frequently when migration is discussed, a political perspective is given priority, perhaps one that takes the point of departure that migrants are problematic and need to be integrated, as well as possibly assimilated. We specifically want to avoid that. Therefore, we attempt to keep to academic discussions about what is known and what we can know and, further, as often as possible, highlight perspectives from the migrants' own experiences.

We now turn to the task of establishing the vocabulary, which might be more problematic than first reckoned.

1.3 Migrants and Migration

In 2016, the International Organization for Migration (IOM, part of the UN) defined a migrant as follows:

> …any person who is moving or has moved across an international border or within a State away from his/her habitual place of residence, regardless of: (1) the person's legal status; (2) whether the movement is voluntary or involuntary; (3) what the causes for the movement are; or (4) what the length of the stay is.

This broad definition of a migrant makes most larger cities in the world cities of migrants due to urbanisation. Such a definition is too broad for this book and possibly also for the IOM, which has developed its definition over the years (www.iom.int). We focus on migrants who cross international borders with the intention of staying longer than for a visit or a holiday. Further, we mainly look at migration from non-European countries, although to that we are not entirely faithful.

In their seminal book, *The Age of Migration*, Stephen Castles et al. (2014) argue that contemporary international migration has six broad new tendencies. The *globalisation of migration* implies that more places are affected by migration and are becoming interdependent on each other; further, the origins of migrants have diversified. The *changing direction of dominant migration flows* have markedly affected Europe, which was a continent of emigration until WWII. Now European emigration is marginal compared to immigration. The *differentiation of migration* means that migration to many places now consists of a range of different types instead of being dominated by a single motivation, like labour migration. The *proliferation of migration transition* highlights an increase in the volume of migration to states where migrants remain for extended periods without, however, intending to stay. The *feminisation of labour migration* emphasises that women are increasingly making up a significant sector of labour migrants. The *growing politicisation of migration* suggests that migration is gradually becoming a pressing item on local, regional, state and interstate agendas, leading to political debate, restrictions, regulations, treaties and new opportunities. Thus, it is inevitable that contemporary societies as well as individual lives are affected by international migration.

Evidently, the experiences of migration are very different. Some migrants are privileged, legally maintaining economic assets and social prestige. For others, migration changes almost everything including social standing, financial and political status and networks. Migrants may encounter racism, hatred for the religion they are assumed to practise and other forms of stereotyping, discrimination or hostility connected to how they are classified, which are often experienced as horrifying and hurtful. Yet they may also experience generosity and welcoming and positive treatment and most encounter every variety of reception.

Nicola Magnusson coined the term *refugeeship* in her PhD dissertation (2011), using discursive social psychology as the main structuring theory. The concept signals the transformation that people go through, starting from the moment when they acutely feel the urge to leave, a decision that will change the narratives about them – both their own and others – probably for the rest of their lives. Refugeeship means the repositioning of identity in relation to 'home', as experience is embodied. Similarly, we can talk about migrantship identity. The experience of migration tends to affect individuals and families – but also societies – for a very long time. Therefore, an essentialist definition of migration may not encompass all the social consequences. We want to emphasise that migration, identity building and reactions to migration are processes. Change should be expected over time.

Thus, we will not proceed from a specific definition of migration. The IOM's open definition and our above-specified reservations and interests will serve as guidelines. Rather, by showing the varying and complex ways migration is connected to religion, we aim to challenge, broaden and deepen the understanding of what both migration and religion can be. This said, we still need some basic foundations, so we should point out that our understanding of migration is related to the concept of international mobility and movement – transnational, global and circular – and includes the mobility of people as well as of goods and ideas.

1.4 Religion

Connecting religion to migration, some clarification about what can be meant by religion may also be useful. First, and maybe most importantly, our understanding of religion aligns with methodological agnosticism, a debated but mostly accepted way to understand and study religion within the sociology of religion (e.g., Porpora, 2006). Methodological agnosticism means that religion is studied as a this-worldly social phenomenon using scientific, non-confessional methods and theories. Thus, we do not make religious truth claims and no religion will be treated as more correct than any other.

1.4 Religion

Obviously, there are religious and theological explanations for some of the social phenomena with which this book is concerned, but these are not our epistemological departure points. Here, religion is understood as assemblages of social and cognitive reactions to an assumed transcendence (or whatever metaphor is appropriate for different religious understandings), and their implications in worldly life. This can be on an individual level, on the way people believe, order and live their lives in relation to the assumed transcendence, or on different group levels, or organised and shared ways of believing and living in relation to this assumed transcendence. On a macro level, it is about how society is organised and relates to religious traditions, but also how society relates to religious groups and to religious individuals, which can refer to a single nation, international relations or even the global level. Two simple examples of the latter are the social and theological reach of the Catholic Church or the fact that there is a global coordination of the teachings of the Muslim Ismaili faith, coordinated from Canada and using up-to-date social media tools.

There is a critique raised against the use of 'religion' as a category that points out its connection to knowledge production in European imperial and colonial states. According to this critique, the concept is seen as a Christo-centric conceptualisation of the vast and complex diversity of 'life worlds', traditions and practices. Thus, religion as a category hampers our understanding by imposing certain structures and logics on people's life worlds, traditions and practices, and at times, in fact, constructing religions out of loose and diverse beliefs, like *one* Hinduism (e.g., Fitzgerald, 2007; King, 1999). Undoubtedly, the term religion has a fascinating history, and it is a fact that European Christianity has – politically and emically – supplied the default understanding for a very long time. This is likely also true in much academic writing; however, that has not prevented many scholars within the broad field of religious studies upholding an inclusive, open and less fixed understanding of the term. Further, many words have troubled histories (democracy, politics, culture, state, class, civilisation, etc.), but can still be re-forged to serve more inclusive perspectives. The critique of 'religion' has failed to present acceptable alternative ways forward; thus, in this book we stick to religion as a concept.

1.4.1 Religion and Secularisation in Europe

A number of countries in Europe have endeavoured to separate religion from the state as part of the shaping of secular state politics. Comparing the number of European states professing a religion (using the juridical definition) in 1900 with 2000, only the Netherlands (out of 45), was proclaimed secular in 1900, while 13 countries were formally secular in 2000 (Madeley, 2009). Several others, like Finland, Denmark and Iceland, retain an official religion, but are, in most aspects, *de facto* secular in legislation. The trend of political secularisation has been consistent for decades and there is every reason to believe that it will continue in the foreseeable future.

The differentiation between state and religion is also related to a general decrease in religious belonging and religious practices in society among the citizens of European countries, a degree of secularisation often described as particular to Europe, and thus different to many non-European societies. In some sense, this is true. Let us look at some figures from the twentieth century. In Sweden, belief in God has declined from being held by 80 percent of the population (1947) to 45 percent (2001) – the lowest in Europe – while the belief in a god in Canada has dropped from 95 to 88 percent in the same time period. In Brazil comparable figures are 96 and 99 percent and in India 98 and 94 percent. The typical European figure by country would be between 60–70 percent. Still, some countries like Japan have even lower figures than Sweden, 35 percent in 2001, likely due to the question being about belief in God rather than a transcendental world; God is a problematic concept in Japan. In Belgium, service attendance has dropped from 52 percent in 1970 to 5 percent in 1998. Even in a country like Ireland it has dropped from a 91 percent attendance in 1970 to 65 percent in 1998 (Norris & Inglehart, 2011). The figures indicate a general development that may change any time, yet the situation is more complex than these figures express; we return to this later in this chapter.

In sociology of religion, these changes are understood as processes of secularisation and – closely related – modernisation. Intertwined with this are the ideologies of modernism and secularism which do not see religions as a necessary or even appropriate part of modern, secular national states and which dominated politics and public debate in many European countries during the 19th and 20th centuries. This is still largely the case in the twenty-first century, although, as debates have changed, some intellectuals now talk about a post-secular society (Habermas, 2005). Nonetheless, due to the secularism drive, religions and individual religious belonging, practices and beliefs are protected by laws in many European countries, most commonly in freedom of religion acts and anti-discrimination laws but also in laws privileging religious organisations, for example through tax exemptions (Byrnes & Katzenstein, 2006). Societies vary in their relations to religion and there are normative aspects connected to these variations.

Many migrants reaching Europe after WWII have arrived from societies where religions hold other positions in society, often more influential or integrated ones. Yet not even that can be taken for granted, as some societies promote secularism, and some migrants, not least European-inspired elites, may have lived European-style secularism more consistently than most Europeans or are refugees because of a committed Marxist or atheist stance or as members of discriminated against or outlawed religious minorities.

Religious beliefs can influence every part of people's lives. The way life, society and persona are understood may all relate to religious beliefs, at times primarily so. Religious beliefs may shape meaning and explain why things happen, have happened and will happen, and can in this way act as a framework for migrants to understand the migrant situation (e.g., Porobić, 2012; McGuire, 2008; Hirschman, 2004). Yet they might also comprise a bothersome heritage difficult to compartmentalise or even leave behind (e.g., Enstedt et al., 2019; Otterbeck, 2010).

In this book, we mainly cover well-established, institutionalised religions that are organised into religious denominations, organisations, communities and groups. We are aware of ongoing religious transformations in contemporary Western societies, from organised religion to more private spirituality, changes that affect large sectors of the population (e.g., Parsons, 2018; Heelas & Woodhead, 2004); however, the research on migration and religion from which we draw has been almost entirely on organised religion. When appropriate, we point out alternatives.

1.5 Religion and Migration

Migration is one of the most distinctive social phenomena in Europe today, and one that reveals a great deal about contemporary European societies. Relating religion to migration allows us to understand European immigration better, but it also makes it possible to learn more about religion in general. This latter aspect has to do with understanding migration as social mobility; it is about a move from one position to somewhere else. What happens with religion in a new situation? Do key features and structures become visible at times of change?

The book shows how social aspects from legislation to cityscapes transform as the result of religious change due to migrations. We touch on how religion affects migration – for example, when people seek the advice of religious specialists about if, and when, to migrate or when someone's religious conviction makes them migrate to spread their religion – but our focus is on how migration affects religion, keeping in mind that other forces than migration change societies. Studying religion as a social phenomenon, we can also observe that religions change over time even without migration: for example, as a result of movements from the countryside and small towns to cities (e.g., AlSayyad & Massoumi, 2011; Schiffauer, 1990), particularly industrialisation and urbanisation in nineteenth-century Europe, which had a huge impact on religion (McLeod, 1997). Moreover, in many European countries, religion continues to have a larger social impact in smaller towns than in larger cities, although international immigration to Europe seems to change this process as we can observe a partial increase of religious practices and active organisations in urban centres in Europe (e.g., Goodhew & Cooper, 2019; Berking et al., 2018; Anderson, 2013).

Changes in religion may also depend on the type of international migration. We know that strong transnational ties are maintained in relation to religion (e.g., Mooney, 2009; Lorentzen et al., 2009; Levitt, 2007), and that temporary migration, circle migration or intra-corporate migration have lower impact on the establishment of religious organisations and religious premises (e.g., Nielsen & Otterbeck, 2016). Reasons for migration also most certainly affect religion; fleeing because of one's religiosity or moving between two countries with similar religious contexts and being vaguely religious, probably affect people's religiosity in different ways (e.g., Saunders et al., 2016).

A substantial part of immigration to Europe is from former colonies to the former colonial centre – not least because of language competence, and contacts – and involves considerable political, economic and social tension, on state, group as well as individual levels. It is marked by the lingering complexities of colonialism that can manifest itself in racism, discrimination, violence, unfair economic relations between countries and the knowledge that the wealth of the former colonial powers has been acquired at the expense of the colonies. The cognitive maps inherited from colonialism may lead to stereotypes (on all sides) about the other (e.g., Keaton, 2006; Pryce, 1974) but may also be challenged by people with inclusive agendas and mindsets. The psychological wish to conquer, or be accepted, is well described in several novels with migration themes, and is part of this structural inequality that is difficult to erase or set aside (e.g., Salih, 2003; Rushdie, 1988).

Evidently, as migrants are people participating in socio-economic contexts, the character of migration and religion changes over time, as we demonstrate. Unfortunately, this will also eventually make this book outdated and in need of a new edition.

1.6 The Complicated Task of Finding Things Out

Below we caution against hastily construed knowledge about migration and religion by questioning some of the very basics of our assumed knowledge. First, we discuss how to establish that changes in religion are due to migration and not temporal factors; the religiosity of youth, for example, often differs from that of elders. Hypothetically, religion in European countries would not have been the same nowadays as in the twentieth century even if there had not been any migration at all; there are many other things in society that change. To be able to discuss this, we must decide what aspects of religion we are studying and the social level on which we are studying it.

If we want to investigate – on a meso level – whether, due to migration, there are fewer or more religious organisations in a country today than before, we must start by finding out if there is a difference compared to, say, 10 or 20 years ago – yet even this seemingly simple task may prove tricky. Registers on religious organisations may provide opportunities to assess whether there has been an increase or a decrease in established groups ('Is there a change in the number of Pentecostal groups?') or in the number of religions/denominations ('Are there Christian charismatic groups that were not here before or are no longer here?'). However, there may be religious organisations that are not registered as religious and religious communities not registered at all. For example, 144 Muslim communities were registered in Sweden in 2017, but there were simultaneously over 700 NGOs that included Islam or Muslims in their name (Sorgenfrei, 2018: 223).

If there have been changes, is migration the reason? We may find that the number of groups is the same as before but this could still be the result of immigration;

society might have had fewer religious organisations without immigration due to secularisation and a loss of interest in organised religion over time. During recent decades in Sweden, so-called protestant free churches have lost many adherents and that has led to the merging of groups and decreasing numbers (not due to immigration); at the same time, the number of orthodox churches has increased (due to immigration).

How do we decide if immigration is the root cause for the increase in orthodox churches, but not for the decrease of protestant free churches? This can be done by finding out if immigrants belong to these churches (micro level). Yet this is difficult in many European countries due to legal restrictions on registering people's religious belonging or because membership registers kept by religious organisations may not be official or may not include information on members' immigration history. Information on immigrant backgrounds among members in religious organisations can at times be estimated by the organisations themselves but this may also be troublesome as we seldom can control how these numbers are generated.

Generally, it is difficult to find statistics covering the religious background of migrants; therefore, researchers tend to use so-called origin proxy. This includes gathering information on people's religious belonging in their country of origin and assuming that emigrants comprise an average sample of this population. There are, however, many difficulties with such statistics, one being that information about religious belonging is often estimated, and, in fact, a hot political potato in many states. It may be difficult, sometimes impossible, to discover the size of minority religious groups, such as the number of Copts in Egypt. Moreover, it is not always a religious average that emigrates from a country; indeed, often religious minorities are more likely to emigrate. Further, belonging to a religious group in the country of emigration is not necessarily followed by belonging in the country of immigration (research rather shows that is not). And, on top of that, who is to decide which groups are to be counted as religious? Alevis, for example, make up a fair part of Turkey's population and are also a large group among the migrants from Turkey. Some of them consider Alevism a religious belonging, but others see it as primarily a cultural identity that may or may not include being Muslim (e.g., Özkul & Markussen, 2022).

Below we present a specific example of what calculations of religious belonging may look like. In Sweden, the number of Muslims is estimated to be between 190,000 (figures from 2018, *SST Yearbook*, 2020) and 800,000, depending on who is writing. The first figure is based on membership in Muslim organisations given state grants, larger figures are estimations based on, at best, former citizenship and the assumed percentage of Muslims coming from a specific country. Authors rarely explain the logic behind their estimates. It is generally unclear whether figures relate only to people with Swedish citizenship, or include people with permanent or only temporary residence, or even people who have recently applied for asylum. Mostly we are not told if converts to Islam or people who have left Islam are included or excluded; nor are we informed if children born in Sweden are included or whether children with one nominally Muslim parent and one non-Muslim parent are accounted for. And that does not cover all possible problems. For example, there are Muslims with Swedish citizenship who live outside Sweden; are they part of the figures provided (see also Thurfjell & Willander, 2021)?

Terms like 'religious affiliation', 'religious belonging' and 'religious preferences' are difficult to substantiate. 'Belonging' signals old-style worldviews, as if people are owned by religious groups. 'Affiliation' implies membership in a group, while 'preferences' implies an active role for the individual and may contain bricolage solutions of affiliations to different groups in different situations. A concept particularly favoured by Otterbeck (2010, 2015) is 'religious family background' as it avoids drawing any premature conclusion about peoples' relations to such backgrounds. After all, it is quite common for people to participate in order to maintain community contacts, as Danièle Hervieu-Léger (2006) has pointed out. It should be clear from above that the ways migrants, like everyone else, relate to religions, vary (see also *The Swiss Metadatabase of Religious Affiliation in Europe (SMRE)*, 2021, https://www.smre-data.ch/). Thus, in research, you must explain what you mean more precisely when you estimate that 4 percent of a population is, for example, Hindu. Do not take statistics on religion at face value. Interrogate them and, if possible, create your own, according to your own methodology.

We may also want to know how people's religion changes due to migration (religion on a micro level), keeping in mind that religious beliefs and practices can have tremendous importance for people in relation to migration: suggesting if and when to migrate, and where and how to learn prayers and find amulets to safeguard the traveller; prompting promises to a god to do good or make offerings if arriving safely; providing information on how to keep in contact with local spiritual centres, religiously powerful people left behind and important contacts during and after the actual migration; even prompting some migrants to change their religion upon arrival in a new country. For many, migrantship is deeply intertwined with religion, an aspect that frequently gets overlooked in migration studies (e.g., Straut-Eppsteiner & Hagan, 2016).

But how should this be researched? Ideally, we should start by asking people about their religiosity before and after they migrate, yet this requires us to know beforehand that specific people will migrate and having the opportunity to ask them again after migration, which is very rarely the case. Another way is to ask – after migration – about religiosity before and after, bearing in mind all the difficulties with recollection and tactical answers when being interviewed (e.g., Van Tubergen, 2013; Van Tubergen & Sindradóttir, 2011; Connor, 2008).

On an aggregated level, we can compare religiosity between a group of people that have not migrated and a comparable group that have and investigate differences in religiosity between them. The difficulty with this is to find comparable groups, but it can be done (Hamberg, 2000). We can also compare religiosity among similar groups of immigrants that have stayed for different periods of time in the same country, which will make it possible to not only include place but also time in understanding how migration influences religion (e.g., Maliepaard et al., 2012).

This leads us to an important perspective related to the phenomenon of religion and migration, namely, integration.

1.7 Religion, Migration and Integration

In migration studies, to be integrated is to be part of a society. Often researchers distinguish between 'assimilation' (effacement of prior group characteristics), 'integration' (merging with the new society without giving up central characteristics), and 'segregation' (isolating as a group from others in society). This division serves a didactic function but does not help researchers in search of a more nuanced understanding. Further, the concepts are often politicized and people from different strands will insist that one or other is the better option, when aspects of all three strategies are often required or observable. Regardless of whether you are a migrant or not, integration processes orchestrate changes that affect most people in a society, although critics of integration debates have pointed out the skewed power balance between immigrants and the established who discursively decide what integration should be and frequently move the goalposts. Some argue that this disqualifies integration as an analytical concept (e.g., Schinkel, 2018); thus, operating with the simple idea of a single overall *integration process* may become counterproductive in research. It makes sense to, at least, distinguish between economic, legal, educational, political, social, cultural and religious integration/assimilation/segregation processes.

For example, European states demand legal assimilation, not integration, of immigrants, which means paying taxes, declaring yearly income, following traffic laws and so on. Yet, due to international agreements and the legal principle of comity, marriage contracts are respected when already entered into legally in the country of origin. In most countries, migrants who are not citizens in the new country of residence may further be divorced according to the law of the country of origin. Not even legal assimilation demands are absolute but must be investigated even more specifically.

Every European country provides different demands, conditions and possibilities for migrants, who are, in turn, tactical about preserving what they think is essential. For example, researchers have noted that while quite a few European states allow imams to oversee marriage contracts to register a marriage before the state, Muslims may not divorce according to Islamic family law if the marriage is registered in these countries. A way of allowing Islamic law to regulate Muslim marriages in European countries is not to register a marriage before the state, but instead sign a private contract that is accepted as a valid marriage before the community. Then divorce can be settled according to tradition and inheritance may be regulated with a will. Methods of avoiding adherence to the pertinent laws while still remaining legal are manifold (e.g., Bowen, 2016).

Formal registration of religious organisations and membership in them illustrate how diverse these integration processes can be. For example, baptism has traditionally been the way a person becomes Catholic, and she or he can thereafter choose to identify as this or not. In cases where membership in a religious organisation also rests on fees – a very common way in western Europe to organise religious minorities – membership becomes less optional. Consequently, religious organisations adapt to the organisational structures of the country in which they operate and change the traditional premises for religious belonging. So, what do people do who are baptised in the country of origin and want to stay Catholic in their new country of residence, but do not want to pay a fee for participation?

The processes of integration related to religion also require an awareness of the processes of secularisation and modernisation mentioned above, and the connected normative understanding of them.

1.8 Religion and Migration from an Intersectional Perspective

To study religion as a social phenomenon in relation to migration cannot be done without including other social aspects such as gender, ethnicity and age (e.g., Saunders et al., 2016). Gender has always been closely related to religions which mostly contain gender systems in which women almost always have a structurally subordinated position to men, evidenced in institutions such as marriage, gendered leadership and male dominance in interpreting religious scriptures, and particularly important if migration is between countries with clear differences in gender equality or roles (e.g., Okin Moller, 1999). We also find that women are normally measured as more religious – or possibly more invested in the religious – than men in terms of religious belonging, beliefs and practices, which should also be taken into consideration in studies about migration and religion (e.g., McGuire, 2008; Stark, 2004).

Ethnicity is often intertwined with religion to the point that separation risks becoming artificial. Being Jewish or Druze are obvious examples of this, but so is being Palestinian and adhering to an Abrahamic religion. Ethnicity and religion are frequently interlaced in minority politics and diaspora identities (e.g., McGuire, 2008: 199f; Kumar, 2004; Ebaugh & Chafetz, 2000; Kashima, 1977; Glazer & Moynihan, 1970).

Age is also important. We know that the configuration of religiosity changes over a life span and differs according to cohort (e.g., Beit-Hallahmi & Argyle, 1997), which should be taken into consideration in relation to migration. As mentioned, migration studies are primarily about changes in place, but may also include time. It is common to compare the religiosity of immigrants and their children to measure changes in religion and its practice due to migration (e.g., Jacob & Kalter, 2013; Raj, 2000; Roof & Manning, 1994), whereupon one must be aware of when the first generation migrated (cohort), how old they were when they migrated (age) and of course their religiosity before and after migration. This is also the case for the immigrants' children: how long have they lived in the country of settlement (cohort) and how old are they now (age)? If the statistics are good enough, we should also take note of the composition of the groups regarding, for example, gender, education and economic class.

Thus, anyone who wants to study migration and religion seriously will have to be attentive to several factors (including some not yet mentioned like class and sexual identity). Unfortunately, we do not always have the luxury of such data, which should not hinder studies, only call for cautious conclusions. Luckily, much has already been done that can support interpretations and help formulate ideas. We now turn to that rich research.

References

Alimia, S. (2019). Performing the Afghanistan–Pakistan border through refugee ID cards. *Geopolitics, 24*(2), 391–425.
AlSayyad, N., & Massoumi, M. (Eds.). (2011). *The fundamentalist city? Religiosity and the remaking of urban space*. Routledge.
Anderson, A. H. (2013). *To the ends of the earth: Pentecostalism and the transformation of world Christianity*. London: Oxford University Press.
Beit-Hallahmi, B., & Argyle, M. (1997). *The psychology of religious behaviour, belief and experience*. London: Routledge.
Berking, H., Steets, S., & Schwenk, J. (Eds.). (2018). *Religious pluralism and the city: Inquiries into postsecular urbanism*. London: Bloomsbury.
Bowen, J. (2016). *On British Islam: Religion, law, and everyday practice in Shariʿa councils*. Princeton: Princeton University Press.
Byrnes, T. A., & Katzenstein, P. J. (Eds.). (2006). *Religion in an expanding Europe*. Cambridge: Cambridge University Press.
Castles, S., de Haas, H., & Miller, M. J. (2014). *The age of migration: International population movements in the modern world* (5th ed.). Houndsmills: Palgrave, Macmillan.
Connor, P. (2008). Increase or decrease? The impact of the international migratory event on immigrant religious participation. *Journal for the Scientific Study of Religion, 47*(2), 243–257.
Ebaugh, H. R., & Chafetz, J. S. (2000). *Religion and the new immigrants: Continuities and adaptations in immigrant congregations*. Walnut Creek, CA: Altamira.
Enstedt, D., Larsson, G., & Mantsinen, T. T. (Eds.). (2019). *Handbook of leaving religion*. Leiden: Brill.
Fitzgerald, T. (2007). *Discourse on civility and barbarity: A critical history of religion and related categories*. Oxford: Oxford University Press.
Glazer, N., & Moynihan, D. P. (1970 [1963]). *Beyond the melting pot: The Negroes, Puerto Rican, Jews, Italians, and Irish of New York City*. Cambridge: The M.I.T. Press.
Goodhew, D., & Cooper, A.-P. (Eds.). (2019). *The desecularization of the city: London's churches, 1980 to the present*. London/New York: Routledge/Taylor and Francis.
Habermas, J. (2005). *Zwischen Naturalismus und Religion: Philosophische Aufsätze*. Frankfurt am Main: Suhrkamp.
Hamberg, E. (2000). *Livsåskådningar, religion och värderingar i en invandrargrupp: En studie av sverigeungrare*. CEIFO skriftserie nr. 85, Stockholm.
Heelas, P., & Woodhead, L. (2004). *The spiritual revolution: Why religion is giving way to spirituality*. Oxford: Blackwell.
Hervieu-Léger, D. (2006). The role of religion in establishing social cohesion. In K. Michalski (Ed.), *Conditions of European solidarity, vol. II: Religion in the new Europe*. Budapest: Central European University Press.
Hirschman, C. (2004). The role of religion in the origins and adaptation of immigrant groups in the United States. *International Migration Review, 38*(3), 1206–1233.
Insoll, T. (Ed.). (2020). *The Oxford handbook of ritual and archaeology*. Oxford: Oxford University Press.

Jacob, K., & Kalter, F. (2013). Intergenerational change in religious salience among immigrant families in four European countries. *International Migration, 51*(3), 38–56.

Kashima, T. (1977). *Buddhism in America: The social organisation of an ethnic religious institution*. Westport, CT: Greenwood Press.

Keaton, T. D. (2006). *Muslim girls and the other France: Race, identity politics, & social exclusion*. Bloomington: Indiana University Press.

King, R. (1999). *Orientalism and religion: Postcolonial theory, India and the 'Mystic East'*. London: Routledge.

Kumar, P. P. (2004). Taxonomy of the Indian diaspora in South Africa: Problems and issues in defining their identity. In K. A. Jacobsen (Ed.), *South Asians in the diaspora: Histories and religious traditions* (pp. 375–392). Leiden: Brill.

Levitt, P. (2007). *God needs no passport: Immigrants and the changing American religious landscape*. New York: The New Press.

Lorentzen, L. A., Gonzalez, J. J., III, Chun, K. M., & Do, H. D. (Eds.). (2009). *Religion at the corner of bliss and nirvana: Politics, identity, and faith in new migrant communities*. Durham: Duke University Press.

Madeley, J. (2009). Religion and the state. In J. Haynes (Ed.), *Routledge handbook of religion and politics*. London: Routledge.

Magnusson, N. (2011). *Refugeeship: A project of justification: Claiming asylum in England and Sweden*. Stockholm: Stockholm University.

Maliepaard, M., Gijsberts, M., & Lubbers, M. (2012). Reaching the limits of secularization? Turkish- and Moroccan-Dutch Muslims in The Netherlands 1998–2006. *Journal for the Scientific Study of Religion, 51*(2), 359–367.

McGuire, M. B. (2008). *Religion: The social context*. Long Grove, IL: Waveland Press.

McLeod, H. (1997). *Religion and the people of Western Europe 1789–1989*. Oxford: Oxford University Press.

Mooney, M. A. (2009). *Faith make us live: Surviving and thriving in the Haitian diaspora*. Berkeley: University of California Press.

Nielsen, J. S., & Otterbeck, J. (2016). *Muslims in western Europe* (4th ed.). Edinburgh: Edinburgh University Press.

Norris, P., & Inglehart, R. (2011). *Sacred and secular: Religion and politics worldwide* (2nd ed.). Cambridge: Cambridge University Press.

Okin Moller, S. (1999). *Is multiculturalism bad for women?* Princeton, NJ: Princeton University Press.

Otterbeck, J. (2010). *Samtidsislam: Unga muslimer i Malmö och Köpenhamn*. Stockholm: Carlsson.

Otterbeck, J. (2015). "I Wouldn't call them Muslims!": Constructing a respectable Islam. *Numen, 62*(2–3), 243–264.

Özkul, D., & Markussen, H. (Eds.). (2022). *The Alevis in modern Turkey and the diaspora: Recognition, mobilization and transformation*. Edinburgh: Edinburgh Studies on Moderns Turkey.

Parsons, W. B. (2018). *Being spiritual but not religious: Past present future(s)*. London: Routledge.

Porobić, S. (2012). *Resilience and religion in a forced migration context: A narrative study of religiousness as a resilience factor in dealing with refugee experiences from a post-migration perspective of Bosnian refugees in Sweden*. PhD thesis, Lund University.

Porpora, D. V. (2006). Methodological atheism, methodological agnosticism and religious experience. *Journal for the Theory of Social Behaviour, 36*(1), 57–75.

Pryce, K. (1974). *Endless pressure: Study of West Indian lifestyles in Bristol*. Bristol: Bristol Classical Press.

Raj, D. S. (2000). "Who the hell do you think you are?" Promoting religious identity among young Hindus in Britain. *Ethnic and Racial Studies, 23*(3), 535–552.

Roof, W. C., & Manning, C. (1994). Cultural conflicts and identity: Second-generation Hispanic Catholics in the United States. *Social Compass, 4*(1), 171–184.

References

Rushdie, S. (1988). *The satanic verses*. London: Viking Penguin.
Salih, T. (2003). *Season of migration to the North*. Penguin.
Saunders, J. B., Fiddian-Qasmiyeh, E., & Snyder, S. (Eds.). (2016). *Intersections of religion and migration: Issues at the global crossroads*. New York: Palgrave/Springer.
Schiffauer, W. (1990). Migration and religiousness. In T. Gerholm & Y. G. Lithman (Eds.), *The new Islamic presence in Western Europe* (pp. 146–158). London: Mansell Publishing.
Schinkel, W. (2018). Against "immigrant integration": For an end to neocolonial knowledge production. *Comparative Migration Studies, 6*(31) Online, no page numbers.
Sorgenfrei, S. (2018). *Islam i Sverige: De första 1300 åren*. Myndigheten för stöd till trossamfund.
SST årsbok. (2020). Yearly report from SST. https://www.myndighetensst.se/om-oss/nyheter/nyhetsarkiv-aktuellt/2020-03-18-religioner-i-rorelse%2D%2D-arsbok-2020.html (Visited 22 March 2020).
Stalker, P. (2002). Migration trends and migration policy in Europe. *International Migration, 40*(5), 151–179.
Stark, R. (2004). *Exploring the religious life?* Baltimore/London: The John Hopkins University Press.
Straut-Eppsteiner, H., & Hagan, J. (2016). Religion as psychological, spiritual, and social support in the migration undertaking. In J. B. Saunders, E. Fiddian-Qasmiyeh, & S. Snyder (Eds.), *Intersections of religion and migration: Issues at the global crossroads* (pp. 49–70). New York: Palgrave/Springer.
The Swiss Metadatabase of Religious Affiliation in Europe (SMRE). (2021). https://www.smre-data.ch/ (Visited 17 August 2021).
Thurfjell, D., & Willander, E. (2021). Muslims by ascription: On post-Lutheran secularity and Muslim immigrants. *Numen, 68*(4), 307–335.
Van Tubergen, F. (2013). Religious change of new immigrants in The Netherlands: The event of migration. *Social Science Research, 42*(3), 715–725.
Van Tubergen, F., & Sindradóttir, J. (2011). The religiosity of immigrants in Europe: A cross-National Study. *Journal for the Scientific Study of Religion, 50*(2), 272–288.

Open Access This chapter is licensed under the terms of the Creative Commons Attribution 4.0 International License (http://creativecommons.org/licenses/by/4.0/), which permits use, sharing, adaptation, distribution and reproduction in any medium or format, as long as you give appropriate credit to the original author(s) and the source, provide a link to the Creative Commons license and indicate if changes were made.

The images or other third party material in this chapter are included in the chapter's Creative Commons license, unless indicated otherwise in a credit line to the material. If material is not included in the chapter's Creative Commons license and your intended use is not permitted by statutory regulation or exceeds the permitted use, you will need to obtain permission directly from the copyright holder.

Chapter 2
Trends in Research: A Literature Review

In this chapter, we present a literature review ordered as a history of the development of theories on migration and religion, addressing the main works on migration to Europe, adding the influential perspectives developed in relation to migration to North America. As a literature review, it is written in a denser style than the rest of the book; therefore, we end each section with a short summary.

2.1 Early Research (1903–1970s)

Already from the early twentieth century, research on contemporary international migration has commented on religion, not least studies from the USA. Introducing early American immigration (slave-)history, the work by William E. B. Du Bois on African American churches in the US – principally his book *The Negro Church* (1903) – is generally considered the first sociological or social science research on migration and religion (see also Woodson, 1921). Du Bois primarily emphasises the religious affiliation of African Americans during this period as social, and only secondarily as religious. Belonging to these religious communities strengthened African Americans in the fight for rights but it was not religion as beliefs and rituals that led to resistance. Instead, he argues, that it was foremost the social aspects of the congregations that supported the political work for equality. That attentiveness to the social aspects of religious engagement became a typical trait in later studies.

Another example of early immigration research including religion is William Thomas and Florian Znaniecki's (1996) ground-breaking sociological book, *The Polish Peasant in Europe and America*, originally published 1918–1920. Based on life histories, diaries and letters sent between Polish settlers in the US and relatives in Poland, the authors demonstrate how the religious function that parishes had in Poland also was of great importance in the US. However, in the US the parishes came to have more functions – especially social – a change in function of religious organisations due to migration seen in many later studies (see also Harkness, 1921).

Published 10 years later, Richard Niebuhr's book, *The Social Sources of Denominationalism* (1929), describes how Christian denominations in the US can be better understood by focusing on economic, social, racial and political differences, instead of differences in theology or ritual. In one of the chapters, he scrutinises what he calls the churches of the immigrants, claiming that these go through two important processes: a process of accommodation when they become more and more like the already established denominations, and a process of differentiation due to their need to distinguish themselves from other denominations. Both these processes were related to the US context which was, and still is, characterised by competition between the various denominations and the mobility of adherents. To be able to compete, the immigrant churches had to be both recognisable and unique. These two processes, Niebuhr claims, included a shift towards revivalism to attract members, while altered relations between the churches and the state tended to depoliticise immigrant churches. A third change has to do with the language used during sermons or other religious practices: English – which for the second and third generations was the only one they fully understood (accommodation) – or the former mother tongue, bringing with it emotional and nostalgic remembrance (differentiation)? It should be pointed out – as the book does – that the other denominations in the US, established during the 18th and 19th centuries, were also founded by immigrants.

Another early contribution to religion and migration research is *The Religious Aspects of Swedish Immigration: A Study of Immigrant Churches* (Stephenson, 1932). In the study, Stephenson describes how immigrants from Sweden go through changes in religiosity and establish, or join, churches in the US. He also shows the importance of the repatriation, or rather circular migration, to Sweden, leading to the establishment of new churches in Sweden at the end of the nineteenth century and the beginnings of the 20th. He is likely the first to affirm the importance of migration for the development of religion in the sending countries (see also Wolf, 1947).

The Yankee City study from 1930 to 1935 headed by William Lloyd Warner, which resulted in five volumes (Warner, 1959; Warner & Lunt, 1941, 1942; Warner & Srole, 1945; Warner & Low, 1947), is also worth mentioning. The project studied the settlement of ethnic groups and the various social factors in Yankee City, a fictive name for a town in Massachusetts. This study did not focus on religion, yet it clearly shows that religion had an influential role in the social constructions of ethnic groups. Supporting this conclusion, Warner and Srole (1945) demonstrate that religious structures are the first social structures to be formalised after arrival and also those that most strongly preserve the ethnic group. At the same time, they may hinder assimilation. The authors further stress the importance of understanding how the status of religion in the former home country connects with its role in the country of immigration.

Oscar Handlin's historical exposition about immigrants to the US, *The Uprooted* (1951), is another good example of an early study addressing religion. He highlights the importance of religion to the studied people and how it supports integration, and demonstrates that religious denominations adapt to the situation of increasing immigration and end up competing. He further observes that the lack of established leadership created a culture of volunteering and contributing. Handlin is one of the first to notice the transnational aspects of religion; for these immigrants, religion fills an important function when nurturing relations with countries of origin.

Will Herberg's *Protestant – Catholic – Jew* (1955) focuses on how religion is re-created and changed in the US because of migration. Like Du Bois, he argues that a common feature of the title's three religious denominations is that affiliation to them is less about theological than social belongingness, which was of fundamental importance to 'the American way of life' and to becoming an American. Both Handling's and Herberg's studies claim that migration causes losses and difficulties, and that religion plays a crucial role in the establishment of migrants in the new country by providing meaning and group affiliation.

Religion also plays a role in Nathan Glazer and Daniel Patrick Moynihan's influential book on immigration and ethnicity in New York, *Beyond the Melting Pot* (1970 [1963]), in which they relate how, after arriving to New York, Puerto Ricans soon sought out other religious denominations than the Catholic Church, including various Pentecostal congregations. The main reason for this was that they could not identify with the Catholic Church that, at the time, was dominated by the Irish and had no Spanish-speaking priests. This observation stresses, yet again, that group identification was even more important than theology.

Milton Gordon's *Assimilation in American Life: The Role of Race, Religion, and National Origins* (1964) has a similar aim as *Beyond the Melting Pot*. Yet it is broader in scope, with an ambition to say something about America. Gordon explores the social arenas based on ethnicity, religion, race and nationality where assimilation takes place, and constructs theories about assimilation processes. He further presents some empirical examples of these complex assimilation processes by analysing three religious groups (Jews, Catholics and white Protestants) and the African American community, describing how, over time, they have come into being through immigration, and how they relate to national and ethnic belongings. To make the reader aware of the many nuances in an overall assimilation process, Gordon separates between different forms of assimilation: for example, 'identificational', attitudinal, marital and structural assimilation. Someone may thus be assimilated in dress, behaviour and most attitudes but, in structural terms, primarily engage off-work with religious peers. This resonates with our earlier distinction between different types of integration (see Sect. 1.7).

The 1970s saw the emergence of new research on the organisations of Czech, Italian, Irish and Polish Catholic ethno-religious groups as well as Armenian Orthodox, Eastern-European Jewish and Buddhist. The anthology, *Immigrants and Religion in Urban America* (Miller & Marzik, 1977), provides various descriptive examples of the constructions of the foremost Catholic ethno-religious groups in urban America from the late nineteenth century until the 1970s, while Tetsuden Kashima (1977) gives an overview of Japanese Buddhists and their organisations in the US in the book *Buddhism in America: The Social Organisation of an Ethnic Religious Institution*. The author emphasises the ethnic and religious importance of these organisations for Japanese immigrants but foresees a broadening of ethnic groups joining the organisations, concluding, 'If this occurs, Buddhism will indeed become fully Americanized' (p. 220; about Buddhism from this period, see Laymen, 1976).

There are also some examples from the 1960s of European research. Johannis J. Mol's book *Churches and Immigrants: A Sociological Study of the Mutual Effect of Religion and Emigrant Adjustment* (1961) is an attempt to collate European and US research on immigration that includes religion (i.e., Christianity and to some extent Judaism) and to sketch a theory – or rather a model. Mol innovatively includes religion on both an institutional and an individual level in his model while earlier research focuses on religious organisations. However, the empirical verifications for religiosity and the religious needs of the immigrants are vague and, to some extent, the book is theologically biased (Mol, 1961; see also Mol, 1959).

Two other examples of early European research are about West Indians in the UK and their religious belonging and organisation, both as Pentecostal groups and in relation to the majority churches (Calley, 1965; Hill, 1963). In these case studies, problems of integration into British society among West Indians in the UK, not least with the majority churches (such as the Church of England and other non-Pentecostal churches), are seen as explanations for opting out of the latter and joining Pentecostal groups and for the turbulence in the studied West Indian Pentecostal congregations.

A similar study is Kenneth Pryce's PhD thesis, *Endless Pressure: Study of West Indian Life-styles in Bristol* (1974). Pryce investigates how different social structures, called 'life-styles', among the West Indians in Bristol function in processes of adaptation. One important lifestyle is provided by the 'all-black church' of Pentecostal origin, to which many of them belong. The church – the author calls it a sect – provides a social context and a place in which their situation as working class and their experiences of racism can be put aside. Instead, they can take comfort in God and the coming of another world after this life. The church offers social help and provides a sense of community; however, it also offers them ethics and morals seen as desirable by the society from which they have withdrawn.

Hans Mol's studies (1976, 1978, 1985) are based on statistical data, and show how international migration, primarily to Canada and Australia but also Belgium, France, Italy, Holland, the UK and the US, changes the religiosity of individuals. Mol describes the relevance of religion in immigrants' identity constructions. Compared to other studies, these indicate a decline in religiosity among immigrants in the countries of immigration.

2.1.1 Summary

We already find some recurrent topics and trends in these early studies. First and foremost, they emphasise the importance of organised religions for identity and group belonging for immigrants. There is an increasing tendency for religious organisations to take on social network functions in new countries. For many, they become a home away from home. This is crucial for the immigrants' perception of themselves and empowerment. At times, religious commitment is associated with lesser levels of social and cultural integration. When qualitative research is done in these organisations, the positive aspects of religion and religious engagement clearly dominate – religion and religious communities provide moral compasses – but through statistics, other patterns may surface, such as indications of religious decline. Finally, a few studies note that the experiences of migrants may also affect the countries of origin.

2.2 Scholarship in the 1980s and 1990s

2.2.1 American Scholarship

Most of the migration studies from the 1980s and 1990s that included religion relate to the US. Not many studies on the topic were published during the 1980s (see also Kivisto, 1992); however, we find some examples. There was a growing amount of research on the Muslim immigrant population in the US (e.g., Abu-Laban & Suleiman, 1989; Abraham & Abraham, 1983; Waugh et al., 1983) and immigrants with East Asian backgrounds (e.g., Fenton, 1988; Yu, 1988; Lewis, et al., 1988; Shin & Park, 1988; Williams, 1988), a trend that continued into the 1990s in the US (on Islam see, e.g., Haddad & Esposito, 1998; McCarus, 1994; Haddad, 1991; and on Asian religions see, e.g., Yang, 1998, 1999; Numrich, 1996; Rutledge, 1991).

A couple of books providing exceptions to this focus on Islam and Asian religions are about Catholicism in the US and its relations with immigration (e.g., Dolan, 1985; Hennesey, 1981). *The American Catholic Experience* (Dolan, 1985) presents the history of Catholicism in the US from the sixteenth century until 1980s. The author closely examines the emergence of what he from 1860 labels to be an immigrant church, and how this is related to ten different national immigrant groups (Czech, Italian, Irish and Polish, German, French Canadian, Mexican, Slovak, Lithuanian, and Ukrainian groups. The author claims that during the beginning of the twentieth century at least twenty-eight different nationalities were represented in the Catholic Church in the US leading to plurality and dynamics, but also to several problems that needed to be solved to keep the Church together (Dolan, 1985).

Raymond Williams' *Religions of Immigrants from India and Pakistan: New Threads in the American Tapestry* (1988) is mostly about Islam and so-called 'Asian religions' (Buddhism, Hinduism, Jainism, Sikhism), but also includes minor parts on Christians, Jews and Zoroastrians. By choosing the countries of origin as the primary starting point, and not religion, Williams' book is innovative in its approach to the study of religion and immigration. This encourages investigation of how former national contexts and the immigrants' history in the chosen countries influence religious adaptation in the country of settlement, and also the impact of length of stay and local population size. Williams traces four patterns across these religions in processes of adaptation in the US, identifying what he calls an ecumenical pattern, a national pattern, an ethnic pattern and a sectarian pattern – the first being the most inclusive and the last the most restrictive in terms of contacts with others. Regardless of degrees of interaction with the surrounding society, Williams foresees many common problems in holding immigrant religious groups together over time, among them those caused by people's geographical mobility and the difficulties of generating new leadership, maintaining language competence and transmitting religious traditions.

From the mid-1990s, we see an overall increase of studies in the field as it became established as a subfield within migration research (which was also an expanding field at the time). The growing amount of research in the US, including various larger research projects, was accompanied by more theoretical outcomes. Further, such work dealt not only with specific religious traditions, but also topics such as transnationalism and globalisation. One early example of these research projects is the *Pluralism Project* at Harvard University, which started in 1991 under the direction of Diana Eck and is still ongoing (Eck, 1997, 2001, see also https://pluralism.org/). Its aim has been to map, investigate and understand the religious landscape emerging in the US after the Immigration and Nationality Act of 1965.

The New Ethnic and Immigrant Congregations Project (University of Illinois, Chicago, 1993–1997) was another US-based, influential research project from the period. A product of the project, Stephen Warner and Judith Wittner (1998), *Gatherings in Diaspora: Religious Communities and the New Immigration*, incorporates studies of ten different immigrant congregations (including Christian, Muslim, Hindu, Jewish and Rastafarian) in different parts of the US, and shows a broad spectrum of how and why they come into being and how they are upheld. The project recruited researchers who had 'linguistic, religious, or national-origin' in common with each studied group, with the goal of gaining access in ways it was believed would not have otherwise been offered (Warner, 2000: 270). The project brought to the fore features including aspects of identity formation, the reception of new immigrants into the established congregations ('proximal hosts'), congregational adaptation and how congregational differences (gender, generation, cohort) are handled. One of the crucial conclusions from this project was that immigrant congregations tended to adapt, over time, to the institutional forms of Protestant Churches.

This assumption, among many other things, was tested and verified in another large US research project of the 1990s, *The Religion, Ethnicity and New Immigrant Research Project* (1996–99), headed by Helen Rose Ebaugh and Janet Chafetz (Ebaugh & Chafetz, 1999, 2000, 2002; Ebaugh et al., 2001; Yang & Ebaugh, 2001a, b). The project examined thirteen immigrant congregations in the same city (Houston, Texas), using formalised interview guides and observation protocols to facilitate comparison between them. The findings were that gender roles were both upheld and transformed (equalised) and that formal and informal religious structures together provided social services to the immigrants. Further, researchers stressed the importance of majority or minority positions in both the US and the former homelands for congregational strategies and activities. Ebaugh and Yang conclude that three principal processes of change are typical of these congregations:

2.2 Scholarship in the 1980s and 1990s

1. that they are adopting the congregational form in organisational structure and ritual,
2. they are returning to theological foundations as they confront diverse subtraditions and ethnic groups within a religion; and
3. they are reaching beyond traditional ethnic and religious boundaries to include other peoples. (Ebaugh, 2010: 107)

To study transnational ties, a follow up project – *The Impact of Transnational Religious Communities on Immigrant Incorporation in the United States*, (1999–2002) – was launched in which in-depth studies were made of six of the congregations using network analysis. The researchers examined how so-called social remittances of religious items were transferred between individuals with ties to both the sending and receiving countries. They also investigated how practiced religions changed, not only in the US, but also in the country of origin (Yang & Ebaugh, 2001a, b; Hagan & Ebaugh, 2003; for 'social remittances' see Sect. 3.4). Another US research project of the period investigated religious diversity in Atlanta, headed by Gary Laderman (1996).

About this time, Stephen Warner (2000) drew together lessons learnt from the large US-based projects into general principles: (1) Religion is typically salient for migrants; (2) migration is not random with respect to religion; (3) identities – individual and collective – are not primordial but negotiated; (4) Religion in the US is subject to processes of isomorphism – that is, taking on the same form – toward congregationalism; (5) congregations (and other religious institutions) become vehicles or venues of intragroup dynamics. While the first principal can be taken for granted in the context of this book, the second is interesting, as Warner sees religious persecution as an important push factor. He points out that while many migrants come from the Middle East, the numbers of Jews, Bahai and Christians are disproportionately high. Points 3–5 will be discussed in Part Two of the book; here it is enough to stress the role of religion in relation to identity negotiations. Warner further demonstrates that organised religion takes on the forms common in the country of immigration and that such organisations also become sites of negotiations, not only of personal identity.

About this time, other US studies with a transnational focus on religion began to appear. Peggy Levitt is an influential scholar who has presented ideas on how religious expression moves back and forth between the countries of origin and the country of immigration (1998, 1999, 2001). Her book, *The Transnational Villagers* (2001), which is based on in-depth fieldwork among immigrants from Miraflores in the Dominican Republic, describes their religious life in both Boston and Miraflores. She also highlights religious organisations as an important intermediary area where bridges are built between the individual and social institutions, and social interaction takes place.

Transnationalism is further developed in Levitt's *God Needs No Passport* (2007). The study uses large data sets drawn from members of four immigrant religious groups in Boston – Pakistani Muslims, Gujarati Hindu organisations, Irish Catholics and Brazilian Evangelical Protestants – which demonstrate the important role played by religious organisations in their transnational lives (see also Rudolph & Piscatori, 1997).

During this period, US research on religion and migration, just like general migration studies, came to embrace processes of globalisation, including the diaspora concept (e.g., Roy, 2004; Rukmani, 1999; Cohen, 1997).

***

In sum, the sparse US research on migration up until the 1990s was mostly concerned with religious communities and how these could help or hinder migrants in adapting to new societies. There was particular interest in Muslim groups, but also some studies on Catholicism. The focus was largely on history and the success or failure of organisations. It was common for researchers to stress that immigrant religious organisations accept forms that are dominant in the new country and take on new social roles.

During the 1990s we see an increase in well-financed, large research programmes, leading to the establishment of migration and religion as a subfield within migration research. Research came to include more comparative and theoretical studies of congregations, allowing for critical observations on gender and generation. Transnational migration – focusing on the relationship between the receiving society and the migrants' homeland communities – along with globalisation processes and diasporas, also appeared on the research agenda. Studies demonstrated that, in many ways, religions and religious identities are and have been non-territorial, flexible and elastic, and often very important and durable, compared to other social identities.

2.2.2 European Scholarship

To some extent, European migration researchers started to include religion systematically in the 1980s, increasing rapidly in the 1990s, most of which focused on Islam and Muslim immigrants (e.g., Nielsen, 1998; Vertovec & Rogers, 1998; Nonneman et al., 1997; Vertovec & Peach, 1997; Geaves, 1996; Schiffauer, 1991; Shadid & van Koningsveld, 1991). Frank Buijs and Jan Rath (2006: 5) estimate that more than a thousand publications on Muslims in contemporary Europe were written before the beginning of the 2000s, and a vast majority of these are from the 1990s.

The few studies that preceded them were largely produced by scholars writing in French and researching the Muslims of France in the 1980s (e.g., Kepel, 1987; Krieger-Krynicki, 1985), along with a number of pioneering UK publications (e.g., Nielsen, 1981; Anwar, 1980). Some groundbreaking studies of Muslims in Europe can be found in the *Journal of Muslim Minority Affairs* launched in 1979, most of which are descriptive, focusing on the history of a particular religious denomination. Information about religion can also be found in studies on immigrants with Muslim backgrounds, especially in the ethnographic literature on Turkish immigrants in Germany, Netherlands and Sweden from the 1970s and onward (e.g., Sachs, 1983; Waardenburg, 1983; Elsas, 1983).

One of the first influential and widely disseminated publications on Muslims in Europe is *The New Islamic Presence in Western Europe*, first published in 1988 (Gerholm & Lithmann, 1990). The edited book gathers together the leading researchers of the time, covering among other things the institutionalisation of Muslim interests and detailing the development of Qur'an schools, organisations and networks. In it, sociologist John Rex, one of the pioneers of UK immigration research, theorises about immigration, ethnicity and religion, seeing religion not as a subcategory of ethnicity but as an intriguing phenomenon interlaced with ethnicity. He is one of the first to do so.

During the late 1980s and 1990s, the publications on migration, Islam and Muslims addressed various areas such as leadership (e.g., Moreras, 1999), integration (e.g., Shadid & van Koningsveld, 1991), youth (e.g., Vertovec & Rogers, 1998; Jacobson, 1998), globalisation (e.g., Alsayyad & Castells, 1997), education (e.g., Anwar, 1988), law (e.g., Shadid & van Koningsveld, 1995), and space making (e.g., Metcalf, 1996). In the 1990s, research on Islam and Muslim immigrants in Europe primarily paid attention to matters connected with political science, such as integration, institutionalisation, laws, democracy, diversity and multiculturalism and secularity, and, only to a lesser degree, to religion-related topics such as theology, faith, rituals, identity building and traditions among Muslim immigrants.

A substantial trend in European research on Muslims during this period examined authority and individualisation, developing theoretical perspectives that addressed how individual integration processes are intertwined with a renegotiation of the locus of authority (e.g., Peter, 2006; Buijs & Rath, 2006). The argument behind this is that the lack of strong socialising institutions in non-Muslim majority countries force or enable (depending on perspective) Muslim migrants to formulate Islam more freely. This line of inquiry was to form a strong paradigm within research, one still present in the literature from the 2000s and 2010s (e.g., Roy, 2004; Tietze, 2001). However, from 2000 onwards research has, according to Frank Peter (2006), come to include more studies on representatives of Muslim authority, such as imams, preachers and muftis, when explaining the ongoing changes in Muslim communities.

There was some research into other religions, but it was rather sparse; for example, settlements in Europe are included in the US books mentioned above with a globalisation and diaspora perspective (e.g., Cohen, 1997; Rukmani, 1999). During this period, there were publications about, or that included the investigation of, Christian communities in Britain established by immigrants from African countries and the Caribbean (e.g., Kalilombe, 1997; Weller, 1994; Ward, 1989; Howard, 1987) and about Hindus in Britain and the Netherlands (e.g., Shadid & van Koningsveld, 1991). *Religion and Ethnicity: Minorities and Social Change in the Metropolis* (Barot, 1993), with chapters on immigrants and religion in urban settings in the UK, Sweden and the Netherlands, is an early example of an anthology which centres on religion, migration and the city, a theme that becomes more common in the 2010s. Four years later, the book *Transnational Religion and Fading*

States (Rudolph & Piscatori, 1997) was published, which contains a chapter on the Catholic Church as a transnational institution.

The literature on migration, Jews and Judaism is rich and, while largely focused on Jewish migration within Europe, to North America or to Israel (e.g., Lewin-Epstein et al., 1997; Goldstein & Goldstein ,1996), it holds many theoretical ideas on subject formation in modernity and postmodernity, community building, diaspora, transnationalism and globalisation. A fine example is *Jewish Identities in the New Europe* (1994) edited by Jonathan Webber. In it, Webber discusses identifications with national and Jewish identities, especially how the Jewish identity, once a given, is today more fluid, open and up to the individual, while national identities now tend to be seen as given. Subjects such as the authority of rabbis and antisemitism are also addressed in the book.

***

Thus, what separated US and European research at the time was the stronger focus on Islam and Muslim immigrants in the latter. Starting in the 1980s, research on Muslims immigrants really took off in the 1990s, while some researchers were also paying attention to other religious groups. As with the US research, much of the initial focus was on organisations and established religious environments, their history and social functions. Later, topics became broader and, not least, theories on religious authority versus individual autonomy were developed. In hindsight, research questions were often formulated from the concerns of the established in society, and discussed issues connected with integration and multiculturalism.

2.3 European Scholarship from 2000–2010

There was an increase in the amount of research published during the period from 2000 to 2010, with a growing input from Canadian scholars (e.g., Beaman & Beyer, 2008; Bramadat & Seljak, 2005; McLellan, 2004) – too voluminous to be presented here. Instead, with a focus on Europe, we mention some examples of different topics that continued from the 1990s and new areas that appeared.

Research on Islam and Muslim immigrants in Europe dominated academic work on religion and migration during this period, and included areas from the decade before, such as leadership (e.g., Kroissenbrunner, 2001; Schiffauer, 2000), integration (e.g., Martín Muñoz et al., 2003; Maréchal et al., 2003), youth and the second generation (e.g., Jacobsen, 2006; Tietze, 2001) and law (e.g., Cesari, 2010, Roald, 2009). We can also observe the growth of research conscious of gender theory (e.g., Farahani, 2007; Keaton, 2006) and the development of new Islamic ideas (e.g., Otterbeck, 2000; Nielsen, 1999). However, a rather large proportion of research on Muslim immigrants maintained a political science focus, while adding an increasingly politicised angle. Themes such as governance (e.g., Bramadat & Koenig, 2009; Bader, 2007), democracy and law (e.g., Sayed, 2009; Cesari, 2004), multiculturalism and diversity (e.g., Al-Azmeh & Fokes, 2007; Bader, 2003), radicalisation

2.3 European Scholarship from 2000–2010

(e.g., Kühle & Lindekilde, 2010; Neumann, 2009), securitisation (e.g., Kaya, 2009) and Islamophobia (e.g., Allen, 2010; Otterbeck & Bevelander, 2006) exemplify this trend. This led to more polarised research, and research results were frequently both presented and read through a political lens.

Research into religions other than Islam in connection with migration was also becoming more common, producing works on Europe and Buddhism and Buddhists (e.g., Prebish & Baumann, 2002; Baumann, 2000), Christianity and Christians (e.g., Ter Haar, 2008; Roudometof et al., 2006), Hinduism and Hindus (e.g., Jacobsen & Kumar, 2004; Baumann, 2000) and Sikhism and Sikhs (e.g., Singh & Tatla, 2006; Hall, 2002). Books were also published on European Jews and Judaism, but if they touched on migration, it was generally intra-European. These studies are mostly about religious organisations and their relations with the receiving countries in Europe and less about themes such as the organisations' religious traditions or religiosity among their adherents or among immigrants not belonging to religious organisations or majority churches.

Meanwhile, there were two fields that were expanding: comparisons between the situation in the US and Europe (e.g., Chebel d'Appollonia & Reich, 2008; Foner & Alba, 2008; Coward et al., 2000) and the trend in US research from transnational studies to studies with a more global focus; the latter was also possible to relate to the European context, as Europe is part of these processes (e.g., Roudometof et al., 2006; Prebish & Baumann, 2002). Those themes found in research on Islam and Muslims in Europe can also be found in work on other religions and religion in a more general sense, but to a lesser extent. There are publications from the period about authority and leadership (e.g., Währisch-Oblau, 2009), integration and diaspora (e.g., Vertovec, 2000; Coward et al., 2000), youth (e.g., Berry et al., 2006), and gender and generations (e.g., Singh & Tatla, 2006; Cetrez, 2011), but also about specific cities (e.g., Martikainen, 2004). Unfortunately, there is very little research from a political science perspective relating to religions other than Islam touching on subjects such as governance, democracy, multiculturalism and diversity, radicalisation and securitisation. We must keep in mind that the socio-political situations of Muslims – giving due weighting to postcolonial resistance, political Islamism and jihadi extremism – are historically specific, but research on other politicised religious identities and migration would be beneficial, particularly for comparative reasons. While there are a few studies, such as an analysis of Hindutva identity among UK Hindi students (e.g., Raj, 2000), they rarely connect results to migration (for exceptions see Bramadat & Koenig, 2009; Bader, 2003). We also find that the early interest in US research on the importance of religion to immigrants' lives is evident in European studies during the 2000s (e.g., Otterbeck, 2010; Nordin, 2004).

***

Thus, while there was still a clear focus on Muslims, there was also a growing interest in people of other faiths and an increased diversification of perspectives. Rather than making its own theoretical contribution, religion and migration research was increasingly relating to the theories that were already in circulation, with both positive and negative effects. While it connected such research to broader theoretical developments in the social sciences, it also reduced the focus on religious studies questions. All this was also typical of the following decade.

2.4 European and Some American Scholarship from 2010

The number of publications by this period was incalculable, and we start to find book-length, comprehensive overviews of the phenomenon in general (e.g., Ramji & Marshall, 2022; Kivisto, 2014; Connor, 2014; Breton, 2012). There was also a rise in the number of publications written from European perspectives. The presentation below mainly addresses these or publications that include Europe, and only overarching themes are discussed.

A growing number of anthologies were published with themes such as the city (e.g., Goodhew & Cooper, 2019; Berking et al., 2018; Garbin & Strhan, 2017; Becci et al., 2011), which until then had been a somewhat neglected area in migration and religion research. This is surprising, since it is well known that immigrant communities often form in cities, and that immigration to western Europe includes people with higher levels of religious practice than that of the urban population in general. Other areas covered by the anthologies are globalisation (e.g., Cherry & Ebaugh, 2014), gender (e.g., Bonifacio & Angeles, 2010), age (primarily youth) (e.g., Sedgwick, 2015), geographical areas in Europe (e.g., Sideri & Roupakia, 2017; Vilança et al., 2014), integration (e.g., Burchardt & Michalowski, 2015), religious diversity (e.g., Hennekam et al., 2018) and securitisation (e.g., Cesari, 2010). Many but not all of these focus on Islam.

It is not until this decade that we start to see a larger number of studies about religious groups other than Muslims: for example, Buddhists (e.g., Swe, 2013; Borup, 2011), Christians, including a growing number of publications on charismatic/Pentecostal groups (e.g., Nilsson DeHanas, 2016; Kubai, 2014; Burgess, 2011; Knibbe, 2011), Orthodox churches (e.g., Sparre & Galal Paulsen, 2018; Hämmerli & Mucha, 2014), Catholics (e.g., Borup, 2011; Trzebiatowska, 2010), Hindus (e.g., Jacobsen & Sardella, 2020; Broo, 2010), Jews (e.g., Toffell, 2013; Goldin et al., 2019) and Sikhs (e.g., Singh, 2022; Jacobsen & Myrvold, 2011, 2012).

The research on Islam and Muslims was increasingly complemented by new themes. Most important among these was a new focus on creativity among migrants, stressing agency and political consciousness (e.g., Jouili, 2015; Lewis, 2015), everyday lived Islam among migrants (e.g., Toğuşlu, 2015; Dessing et al., 2013), LGBTQI+ individuals and groups pragmatically addressing the role of marginal sexualities in migration (e.g., Tschalaer, 2019; Peumans, 2018), detailed studies of radical organisation and thought (e.g., Inge, 2017; Nesser, 2015), the history of Muslim minorities – the Ahmadiyyas (e.g., Balzani, 2020; Jonker, 2016), the Alevis (e.g., Özkul & Markussen, 2022) and the Ismailis (e.g., Magout, 2020), early migration history in various countries (e.g., Sorgenfrei, 2018), discussion of minority law (e.g., Bowen, 2016), Islamophobia, complemented by whiteness and the racialisation of Muslims (e.g., Jakku, 2018) and, finally, the development of new Islamic ideas (e.g., Hashas, 2019; van Bruinessen & Allievi, 2011).

***

As in former periods, there was a considerable emphasis on religion in relation to other social structures, and less on changes in religious organisations and religious practices, with some exceptions (e.g., Soeffner & Zifonun, 2016; Jeldtoft, 2012), discussed further in Part Three. Islam was still in focus and, although mostly regarded from a more political perspective, some other new areas were included. We also see a growing research interest in other religions and a marked rise in interest in the very formulation of religion and in rituals. The focus on cities and local environments also produced an awareness of the great relevance of socio-economic conditions in neighbourhoods, cities and regions to how immigrants formulate and express religion. Of the utmost importance is the new awareness of, and stress placed on, the complexities of religion to migrants in different subject positions.

2.5 Concluding Remarks

Research on migration and religion has been multidisciplinary, taking place in sociology, anthropology and history of religions; increasingly, however, it has become important in political science, with interest in topics such as the relations between secular states and immigration, and multiculturalism and religion. Religion and migration have been linked to law – when, for example, increasingly pluralistic and global societies challenge, among other things, religious freedom laws, demonstrating how laws are not universal but formed by local contexts and the historical dominance of particular forms of Christianity – and are studied by scholars of legal studies, while religion is also linked to migration in psychology, in trans-generational research and in studies of the role religion can play in traumas that can follow from living in refugeeship.

Even though research on migration and religion has grown during the last decades, it has still a quite limited impact within migration research in and about Europe. For example, there were no sessions at the 2021 IMISCOE (Immigration Migration Research Network) conference with religion as a topic, and out of more than 1000 papers, only 26 included 'religion' (or words related to religion) in the titles; at the 2020 IMISCOE conference a single session out of more than 100 sessions was about religion (see also Ebaugh, 2010). We hope partly to overcome this peripheral position of migration and religion with this book.

As we can see from the above discussion, research on migration and religion is complex and covers a broad gamut of phenomena. Would it not, then, be possible to present an overall theory on migration and religion? We argue that doing so risks missing crucial aspects of relations between them. Instead, in the following, we discuss how to understand religion in relation to migration, providing various examples of research done in accordance with this, delimiting the research done to post WWII and immigration to Europe.

References

Abraham, S., & Abraham, N. (Eds.). (1983). *Arabs in the New World*. Detroit: Wayne State University.
Abu-Laban, B., & Suleiman, M. W. (Eds.). (1989). *Arab-Americans: Continuity and change*. AAUG Press.
Al-Azmeh, A., & Fokes, E. (Eds.). (2007). *Islam in Europe: Diversity, identity and influence*. Cambridge: Cambridge University Press.
Allen, C. (2010). *Islamophobia*. Farnham: Ashgate.
AlSayyad, N., & Castells, M. (1997). *Muslims in Europe or Euro-Islam: Politics, culture, and citizenship in the age of globalization*. Lexington, MA: Lexington Books.
Anwar, M. (1980). Religious identity in plural societies: The case of Britain. *Journal of Muslim Minority Affairs, 2*(2), 110–121.
Anwar, M. (1988). Muslim community and the issues in education. In B. O'Keeffe (Ed.), *Schools for tomorrow: Building walls or building bridges* (pp. 80–100). London: Falmer Press.
Bader, V. (2003). Religious diversity and democratic institutional pluralism. *Political Theory, 31*(2), 265–294.
Bader, V. (2007). The governance of Islam in Europe: The perils of modelling. *Journal of Ethnic and Migration Studies, 33*(6), 871–886.
Balzani, M. (2020). *Ahmadiyya Islam and the Muslim diaspora: Living at the end of days*. Abingdon, Oxon: Routledge.
Barot, R. (Ed.). (1993). *Religion and ethnicity: Minorities and social change in the Metropolis*. Kampen, NL: Kok Pharos Publishing.
Baumann, M. (2000). *Migration, religion, integration: Buddhistische Vietnamesen und hinduistische Tamilen in Deutschland*. Marburg: Diagonal Verlag.
Beaman, L. G., & Beyer, P. (Eds.). (2008). *Religion and diversity in Canada*. Leiden: Brill Academic Publishers.
Becci, I., Burchardt, M., & Casanovas, J. (Eds.). (2011). *Topographies of faith: Religion in urban spaces*. Leiden/Boston: Brill.
Berking, H., Steets, S., & Schwenk, J. (Eds.). (2018). *Religious pluralism and the city: Inquiries into postsecular urbanism*. London: Bloomsbury.
Berry, J. W., Phinney, J. S., Sam, D. L., & Vedder, P. (Eds.). (2006). *Immigrant youth in cultural transition: Acculturation, identity, and adaptation across national contexts*. London: Routledge.
Bonifacio, G. T., & Angeles, V. S. M. (Eds.). (2010). *Gender, religion, and migration: Pathways of integration*. Lanham, MD: Lexington Books.
Borup, J. (2011). *Religion, kultur og integration: Vietnamesere i Danmark*. København: Museum Tusculanums Forlag.
Bowen, J. (2016). *On British Islam: Religion, law, and everyday practice in Shariʿa councils*. Princeton: Princeton University Press.
Bramadat, P., & Koenig, M. (Eds.). (2009). *International migration and the governance of religious diversity*. Montreal: McGill-Queen's University Press.
Bramadat, P., & Seljak, D. (Eds.). (2005). *Religion and ethnicity in Canada*. Toronto: University of Toronto Press.
Breton, R. (2012). *Different gods: Integrating Non-Christian minorities*. Montreal & London: McGill Queen's University Press.
Broo, M. (2010). ISKCON and south Asian Hindus in Finland: Strategies for integration. *Finnish Journal of Ethnicity and Migration, 5*(2), 33–38.
Buijs, F. J., & Rath, J. (2006). *Muslims in Europe: The state of research*. IMISCOE working paper. Universiteit van Amsterdam. https://pure.uva.nl/ws/files/4364118/68548_MuslimsinEurope_Thestateofresearch.pdf (Visited 21 March 2022).
Burchardt, M., & Michalowski, I. (Eds.). (2015). *After integration: Islam, conviviality and contentious politics in Europe*. Wiesbaden: Springer Fachmedien.
Burgess, R. (2011). Bringing Back the gospel: Reverse Mission among Nigerian Pentecostals in Britain. *Journal of Religion in Europe, 4*(3), 429–449.

References

Calley, M. J. C. (1965). *God's people: West Indian Pentecostal sects in England*. Oxford University Press.

Cesari, J. (2004). *When Islam and democracy meet: Muslims in Europe and in the United States*. New York: Palgrave Macmillan.

Cesari, J. (Ed.). (2010). *Muslims in the West after 9/11: Religion, politics, and law*. London: Routledge.

Cetrez, Ö. (2011). The next generation of Assyrians in Sweden: Religiosity as a functioning system of meaning within the process of acculturation. *Mental Health, Religion & Culture, 14*(5), 473–487.

Chebel d'Appollonia, A., & Reich, S. (Eds.). (2008). *Immigration, integration, and security: America and Europe in comparative perspective*. Pittsburgh: University of Pittsburgh Press.

Cherry, S. M., & Ebaugh, H. R. (Eds.). (2014). *Global religious movement across borders: Sacred service*. Burlington: Ashgate.

Cohen, R. (1997). *Global diasporas: An introduction*. London: UCL Press.

Connor, P. (2014). *Immigrant faith: Patterns of immigrant religion in the United States, Canada, and Western Europe*. New York: New York University Press.

Coward, H., Hinnells, J. R., & Williams, R. B. (2000). *The South-Asian religious diaspora in Britain, Canada, and the United States*. New York: SUNY Press.

Dessing, N. M., Jeldtoft, N., Nielsen, J., & Woodhead, L. (Eds.). (2013). *Everyday lived Islam in Europe*. Farnham: Ashgate.

Dolan, J. (1985). *The American Catholic experience: A history from colonial times to the present*. New York: Doubleday & Company.

Du Bois, W. E. B. (1903). *The Negro church*. Atlanta: Atlanta University Press.

Ebaugh, H. R. (2010). Transnationality and religion in immigrant congregations: The global impact. *Nordic Journal of Religion and Society, 23*(2), 105–119.

Ebaugh, H. R., & Chafetz, J. S. (1999). Agents for cultural reproduction and structural change: The ironic role of women in immigrant religious institutions. *Social Forces, 78*(2), 585–612.

Ebaugh, H. R., & Chafetz, J. S. (2000). *Religion and the new immigrants: Continuities and adaptations in immigrant congregations*. Walnut Creek, CA: Altamira.

Ebaugh, H. R., & Chafetz, J. S. (Eds.). (2002). *Religion across borders: Transnational immigrant networks*. Lanham: Altamira Press.

Ebaugh, F., Rose, H., & Pipes, P. F. (2001). Immigrant congregations as social service providers: Are they safety nets for welfare reform? In P. Nesbitt (Ed.), *Religion and social policy* (pp. 95–110). Walnut Creek, CA: AltaMira.

Eck, D. (1997). *On common ground: World religions in America*. Columbia University Press. [CD-ROM].

Eck, D. (2001). *A new religious America: How a 'Christian country' has now become the world's most religiously diverse nation*. San Francisco: Harper.

Elsas, C. (Ed.). (1983). *Identität: Veränderungen kultureller Eigenarten im Zusammenleben von Türken und Deutschen*. Hamburg: Rissen.

Farahani, F. (2007). *Diasporic narratives of sexuality: Identity formation among Iranian-Swedish women*. Stockholm: Stockholm University.

Fenton, J. Y. (1988). *Transplanting religious traditions: Asian Indians in America*. New York: Praeger.

Foner, N., & Alba, R. (2008). Immigrant religion in the US and Western Europe: Bridge or barrier to inclusion? *International Migration Review, 42*(2), 360–392.

Garbin, D., & Strhan, A. (Eds.). (2017). *Religion and the global city*. London: Bloomsbury.

Geaves, R. (1996). *Sectarian influences within Islam in Britain with reference to the concepts of 'Ummah' and 'community'*. Leeds: Department of Theology and Religious Studies, University of Leeds.

Gerholm, T., & Lithmann, Y. (Eds.). (1990 [1988]). *The new Islamic presence in Western Europe*. London: Mansell Publishing.

Glazer, N., & Moynihan, D. P. (1970 [1963]). *Beyond the melting pot: The Negroes, Puerto Rican, Jews, Italians, and Irish of New York City*. Cambridge: The M.I.T. Press.

Goldin, S., Spiro, M., & Ury, S. (Eds.). (2019). *Jewish migration in modern times*. Abingdon, Oxon: Routledge.

Goldstein, S., & Goldstein, A. (1996). *Jews on the move: Implications for Jewish identity*. New York: State University of New York Press.

Goodhew, D., & Cooper, A.-P. (Eds.). (2019). *The desecularization of the city: London's churches, 1980 to the present*. London/New York: Routledge, Taylor and Francis.

Gordon, M. M. (1964). *Assimilation in American life: The role of race, religion, and national origins*. New York: Oxford University Press.

Haddad, Y. Y. (Ed.). (1991). *The Muslims of America*. New York: Oxford University Press.

Haddad, Y. Y., & Esposito, J. L. (Eds.). (1998). *Muslims on the Americanization path?* New York: Oxford University Press.

Hagan, J., & Ebaugh, H. R. (2003). Calling upon the sacred: Migrants' use of religion in the migration process. *International Migration Review, 37*(4), 1145–1162.

Hall, K. D. (2002). *Lives in translation: Sikh youth as British citizens*. Philadelphia: University of Pennsylvania Press.

Hämmerli, M., & Mucha, E. (2014). Innovation in the Russian Orthodox Church: The crisis in the diocese of Sourozh in Britain. In M. Hämmerli & J.-F. Mayer (Eds.), *Orthodox identities in Western Europe: Migration, settlement and innovation* (pp. 291–302). London: Routledge.

Handlin, O. (1951). *The uprooted: The epic story of the great migrations that made the American people*. Boston: Little, Brown and Co.

Harkness, G. (1921). *The church and the immigrant*. George H. Doran Co.

Hashas, M. (2019). *The idea of European Islam: Religion, ethics, politics and perpetual modernity*. London: Routledge.

Hennekam, S., Peterson, J., Tahssain-Gay, L., & Dumazert, J.-P. (2018). Managing religious diversity in secular organizations in France. *Employee Relations, 40*(5), 746–761.

Hennesey, J. (1981). *American Catholics: A history of the Roman Catholic Community in the United States*. New York: Oxford University Press.

Herberg, W. (1955). *Protestant – Catholic – Jew: An essay in American religious sociology*. New York: Doubleday.

Hill, C. S. (1963). *West Indian migrants and the London churches*. London: Oxford University Press.

Howard, V. (1987). A report on Afro-Caribbean Christianity in Britain. In *Community religions project research papers no. 4*. Leeds: The University of Leeds.

Inge, A. (2017). *The making of a Salafi Muslim woman*. Oxford: Oxford University Press.

Jacobsen, C. M. (2006). *Staying on the straight path: Religious identities and practices among young Muslims in Norway*. PhD Thesis, University of Bergen, Norway.

Jacobsen, K. A., & Kumar, P. P. (Eds.). (2004). *South Asians in the diaspora: Histories and religious traditions*. Leiden: Brill.

Jacobsen, K. A., & Myrvold, K. (Eds.). (2011). *Sikhs in Europe: Migration, identities and representations*. Farnham: Ashgate.

Jacobsen, K. A., & Myrvold, K. (Eds.). (2012). *Sikhs across borders: Transnational practices of European Sikhs*. London: Bloomsbury Academic.

Jacobsen, K. S., & Sardella, F. (Eds.). (2020). *Handbook of Hinduism in Europe, volume 2*. Leiden: Brill.

Jacobson, J. (1998). *Islam in transition: Religion and identity among British Pakistani Youth*. London: Routledge.

Jakku, N. (2018). Islamophobia, representation and the Muslim political subject: A Swedish case study. *Societies, 8*(4), 1–17.

Jeldtoft, N. (2012). *Everyday lived Islam: Religious reconfigurations and secular sensibilities among Muslim minorities in the West*. PhD Thesis, Faculty of Theology, University of Copenhagen.

Jonker, G. (2016). *The Ahmadiyya quest for religious progress: Missionizing Europe 1900–1965*. Leiden: Brill.

Jouili, J. S. (2015). *Pious practice and secular constraints: Women in the Islamic revival in Europe*. Stanford: Stanford University Press.

Kalilombe, P. (1997). Black Christianity in Britain. *Ethnic and Racial Studies, 20*(2), 306–324.

Kashima, T. (1977). *Buddhism in America: The social organisation of an ethnic religious institution*. Westport, CT: Greenwood Press.

References

Kaya, A. (2009). *Islam, migration and integration: The age of securitization*. New York: Palgrave Macmillan.

Keaton, T. D. (2006). *Muslim girls and the other France: Race, identity politics, & social exclusion*. Bloomington: Indiana University Press.

Kepel, G. (1987). *Les Banlieues de l'Islam*. Paris: Editions du Seui I.

Kivisto, P. (1992). Religion and the new immigrants. In W. H. Swatos (Ed.), *A future for religion? New paradigms for social analysis*. Thousand Oaks, CA: Sage.

Kivisto, P. (2014). *Religion and immigration: Migrant faiths in North America and Western Europe*. Polity.

Knibbe, K. E. (2011). Nigerian missionaries in Europe: History repeating itself or a meeting of modernities. *Journal of Religion in Europe, 4*(3), 471–487.

Krieger-Krynicki, A. (1985). *Les musulmans en France*. Paris: Maisonneuve Larose.

Kroissenbrunner, S. (2001). *Türkische Imame in Wien*. Vienna: Forschungsbericht am Institut für Konfliktforschung.

Kubai, A. (2014). Accommodation and tension: African Christian communities and their Swedish hosts. In H. Vilança, E. Pace, I. Furseth, & P. Pettersson (Eds.), *The changing soul of Europe: Religions and migrations in Northern and Southern Europe* (pp. 149–172). Farnham: Ashgate.

Kühle, L., & Lindekilde, L. (2010, January). *Radicalization among young Muslims in Aarhus*. Centre for Studies in Islamism and Radicalisation (CIR), Department of Political Science, Aarhus University.

Laderman, G. (Ed.). (1996). *Religions of Atlanta: Religious diversity in the centennial Olympic City*. Atlanta: Scholars Press / Oxford University Press.

Layman, E. (1976). *Buddhism in America*. Chicago: Nelson-Hall Publishers.

Levitt, P. (1998). Local-level global religion: The case of US-Dominican migration. *Journal for the Scientific Study of Religion, 37*(1), 74–89.

Levitt, P. (1999). Social remittances: A local-level, migration-driven form of cultural diffusion. *International Migration Review, 32*(4), 926–948.

Levitt, P. (2001). *The transnational villagers*. Berkeley: University of California Press.

Levitt, P. (2007). *God needs no passport: Immigrants and the changing American religious landscape*. New York: The New Press.

Lewin-Epstein, N., Ro'i, Y., & Ritterband, P. (Eds.). (1997). *Russian Jews on three continents: Migration and resettlement*. London: Frank Cass.

Lewis, R. (2015). *Muslim fashion: Contemporary style cultures*. Durham: Duke University Press.

Lewis, R. E., Fraser, M. W., & Pecora, P. J. (1988). Religiosity among Indochinese refugees in Utah. *Journal for the Scientific Study of Religion, 27*(2), 272–283.

Magout, M. (2020). *A reflexive Islamic modernity: Academic knowledge and religious subjectivity in the global Ismaili community*. Baden-Baden: Nomos.

Maréchal, B., Allievi, S., Dassetto, F., & Nielsen, J. (Eds.). (2003). *Muslims in the enlarged Europe: Religion and society*. Leiden: Brill.

Martikainen, T. (2004). *Immigrant religions in local society: Historical and contemporary perspectives in the city of Turku*. Åbo: Åbo Akademi University Press.

Martín Muñoz, G., Castaño, F. J. G., Sala, A. L., & Crespo, R. (2003). *Marroquíes en España: Estudio sobre su integración*. Madrid: Fundación REPSOL.

McCarus, E. (Ed.). (1994). *The development of Arab-American identity*. Ann Abor: University of Michigan Press.

McLellan, J. (2004). Cambodian refugees in Ontario: Religious identities, social cohesion and transnational linkages. *Canadian Ethnic Studies Journal, 36*(2), 101–118.

Metcalf, B. D. (Ed.). (1996). *Making Muslim space in North America and Europe*. London: University of California Press.

Miller, R. M., & Marzik, T. D. (Eds.). (1977). *Immigrants and religion in urban America*. Philadelphia: Temple University Press.

Mol, J. J. (1959). Theoretical frame of reference for the interactional patterns of religion and the adjustment of immigrants. *Research group for European Migrations Problems, Bulletin, 7*(2), 21–43.

Mol, J. J. (1961). Churches and immigrants: A Sociological Study of the Mutual Effect of Religion and Emigrant Adjustment. *Research group for European Migrations Problems, Bulletin, Supplement, 5*, 89.

Mol, H. (1976). *Identity and the sacred: A sketch for a new social-scientific theory of religion*. Oxford: Basil Blackwell.
Mol, H. (1978). *Identity and religion: International, cross-cultural approaches*. London: Sage.
Mol, H. (1985). *Faith and fragility-religion and identity in Canada*. Burlington: Trinity Press.
Moreras, J. (1999). *Musulmanes en Barcelona*. Barcelona: CIDOB Edicions.
Nesser, P. (2015). *Islamist terrorism in Europe: A history*. London: Hurst.
Neumann, P. R. (2009). *Joining Al-Qaeda: Jihadist recruitment in Europe*. Abingdon: Routledge.
Niebuhr, H. R. (1929). *The social sources of denominationalism*. New York: H. Holt.
Nielsen, J. S. (1981). Muslim education at home and abroad. *British Journal of Religious Studies, 3*(3), 94–99, 107.
Nielsen, J. S. (Ed.). (1998). *Christian-Muslim frontier: Chaos, clash or dialogue?* London: Bloomsbury.
Nielsen, J. S. (1999). *Towards a European Islam*. London: Palgrave Macmillan.
Nilsson DeHanas, D. (2016). *London youth, religion, and politics: Engagement and activism from Brixton to Brick Lane*. Oxford: Oxford University Press.
Nonneman, G., Niblock, T., & Szajkowski, B. (Eds.). (1997). *Muslim communities in the new Europe*. London: Ithaca Press.
Nordin, M. (2004). *Religiositet bland migranter: Sverige-chilenares förhållande till religion och samfund*. Lund: Centre for Theology and Religious Studies.
Numrich, P. D. (1996). *Old wisdom in the new world: Americanization in two immigrant Theravada Buddhist temples*. Knoxville, TN: University of Tennessee Press.
Otterbeck, J. (2000). *Islam på svenska: Tidskriften Salaam och islams globalisering*. Stockholm: Almqvist & Wiksell.
Otterbeck, J. (2010). *Samtidsislam: Unga muslimer i Malmö och Köpenhamn*. Stockholm: Carlsson.
Otterbeck, J., & Bevelander, P. (2006). *Islamofobi: En studie av begreppet, ungdomars attityder och unga muslimers utsatthet*. Stockholm: Forum för levande historia.
Özkul, D., & Markussen, H. (Eds.). (2022). *The Alevis in modern Turkey and the diaspora: Recognition, mobilization and transformation*. Edinburgh: Edinburgh Studies on Moderns Turkey.
Peter, F. (2006). Individualization and religious authority in Western European Islam. *Islam and Christian–Muslim Relations, 17*(1), 105–118.
Peumans, W. (2018). *Queer Muslims in Europe: Sexuality, religion and migration in Belgium*. London: I.B. Tauris.
Prebish, C. S., & Baumann, M. (2002). *Westward dharma: Buddhism beyond Asia*. Berkeley: University of California Press.
Pryce, K. (1974). *Endless pressure: Study of West Indian lifestyles in Bristol*. Bristol: Bristol Classical Press.
Raj, D. S. (2000). "Who the hell do you think you are?" promoting religious identity among young Hindus in Britain. *Ethnic and Racial Studies, 23*(3), 535–552.
Ramji, R., & Marshall, A. (Eds.). (2022). *The Bloomsbury handbook of religion and migration*. London: Bloomsbury.
Roald, A. S. (2009). *Muslimer i nya samhällen*. Göteborg: Daidalos.
Roudometof, V., Agadjanian, A., & Pankhurst, J. (Eds.). (2006). *Eastern Orthodoxy in a global age: Tradition faces the twenty-first century*. Walnut Creek: Altamira.
Roy, O. (2004). *Globalized Islam: The search for a new Ummah*. New York: Columbia University Press.
Rudolph, S. H., & Piscatori, J. (Eds.). (1997). *Transnational religion and fading states*. Boulder, CA: Westview Press.
Rukmani, T. S. (Ed.). (1999). *Hindu Diaspora: Global perspectives*. Montreal: The Chair of Hindu Studies, Concordia University.
Rutledge, P. (1991). Strategies for ethnicity in religion: The employment of religious perceptions by Vietnamese people in Oklahoma. *Asian Journal of Theology, 5*(1), 176–185.
Sachs, L. (1983). *Onda ögat eller bakterier: Turkiska invandrarkvinnors möte med svensk sjukvård*. Stockholm: Liber.
Sayed, M. (2009). *Islam och arvsrätt i det mångkulturella Sverige: En internationellt och jämförande studie*. Uppsala: Iustus Förlag AB.

References

Schiffauer, W. (1991). *Die Migranten aus Subay; Türken in Deutschland: eine Ethnographie.* Stuttgart: Klett-Cotta.

Schiffauer, W. (2000). *Die Gottesmänner: Türkische Islamisten in Deutschland.* Frankfurt a. M.: Suhrkamp.

Sedgwick, M. (Ed.). (2015). *Making European Muslims: Religious socialization among young Muslims in Scandinavia and Western Europe.* New York: Routledge.

Shadid, W. A. R., & van Koningsveld, P. S. (Eds.). (1991). *The integration of Islam and Hinduism in Western Europe.* Kampen: Kok Pharos.

Shadid, W. A. R., & van Koningsveld, P. S. (Eds.). (1995). *Religious freedom and the position of Islam in Western Europe: Opportunities and obstacles in the acquisition of equal rights.* Kampen: Kok Pharos.

Shin, E. H., & Park, H. (1988). An analysis of causes of schisms in ethnic churches: The case of the Korean-American churches. *The Sociological Review, 49*(3), 234–248.

Sideri, E., & Roupakia, L. E. (2017). *Religions and migrations in the Black Sea region.* Cham, Switzerland: Palgrave Macmillan.

Singh, J. (2022). Sikh activism in diaspora: Migration and representation. In R. Ramji & A. Marshall (Eds.), *The Bloomsbury handbook of religion and migration* (pp. 25–35). London: Bloomsbury.

Singh, G., & Tatla, D. S. (2006). *Sikhs in Britain: The making of a community.* London: Zed Books.

Soeffner, H.-G., & Zifonun, Darius̆ (Eds.). (2016). *Ritual change and social transformation in migrant societies.* New York: Peter Lang, Academic Research.

Sorgenfrei, S. (2018). *Islam i Sverige: De första 1300 åren.* Stockholm: Myndigheten för stöd till trossamfund.

Sparre, S. L., & Galal Paulsen, L. (2018). Incense and holy bread: The sense of belonging through ritual among Middle Eastern Christians in Denmark. *Journal of Ethnic and Migration Studies, 44*(16), 2649–2666.

Stephenson, G. M. (1932). *The religious aspects of Swedish immigration: A study of immigrant churches.* Minneapolis: The University of Minnesota Press.

Swe, Y. Y. (2013). Mobility encounter: The narratives of Burmese refugees in Norway. *Norwegian Journal of Geography, 67*(4), 229–238.

Ter Haar, G. (2008). Enchantment and identity: African Christians in Europe. *Archives de Sciences Sociales des Religions, 53*(143), 31–48.

Thomas, W. I., & Znaniecki, F. (1996 [1918–1920]). In E. Zaretsky (Ed.), *The Polish peasant in Europe and America, 5 vols.* University of Illinois Press.

Tietze, N. (2001). *Islamische Identitäten: Formen muslimischer Religiosität junger Männer in Deutschland und Frankreich.* Hamburg: Hamburger Edition.

Toffell, G. (2013). From bodies to souls: Jewish youth clubs in the East End of London and the transmission of tradition. In J. Garnett & A. Harris (Eds.), *Rescripting religion in the City: Migration and religious identity in the modern metropolis* (pp. 191–202). London: Ashgate.

Toğuşlu, E. (Ed.). (2015). *Everyday life practices of Muslims in Europe.* Leuven: Leuven University Press.

Trzebiatowska, M. (2010). The advent of the "EasyJet priest": Dilemmas of Polish Catholic integration in the UK. *Sociology, 44*(6), 1055–1072.

Tschalaer, M. (2019). Between queer liberalisms and Muslim masculinities: LGBTQI+ Muslim asylum assessment in Germany. *Ethnic and Racial Studies, 43*(7), 1265–1283.

van Bruinessen, M., & Allievi, S. (Eds.). (2011). *Producing Islamic knowledge: Transmission and dissemination in Western Europe.* London: Routledge.

Vertovec, S. (2000). *The Hindu diaspora: Comparative patterns.* London: Routledge.

Vertovec, S., & Peach, C. (Eds.). (1997). *Islam in Europe: The politics of religion and community.* London: Palgrave Macmillan.

Vertovec, S., & Rogers, A. (Eds.). (1998). *Muslim European youth: Reproducing ethnicity, religion, culture.* Aldershot: Ashgate.

Vilança, H., Pace, E., Furseth, I., & Pettersson, P. (Eds.). (2014). *The changing soul of Europe: Religions and migrations in Northern and Southern Europe.* Farnham: Ashgate.

Waardenburg, J. (1983). The right to ritual: Mosques in The Netherlands. *Nederlands Theologisch Tijdschrift, 37*(3), 253–264.

Währisch-Oblau, C. (2009). *The missionary self-perception of Pentecostal/charismatic church leaders from the global South in Europe: Bringing back the gospel*. Leiden: Brill.
Ward, T. (1989). *Praise the Lord! Black-led churches in Britain*. Birmingham: Centre for Black and White Christian Partnership.
Warner, W. L. (1959). *The living and the dead: A study in the symbolic life of Americans*. New Haven: Yale University Press.
Warner, S. (2000). Religion and new (Post-1965) immigrants: Some principles drawn from field research. *American Studies, 41*(2), 267–286.
Warner, W. L., & Low, J. O. (1947). *The social system of the modern factory. The strike: A social analysis* (The Yankee City series) (Vol. 4). New Haven: Yale University Press.
Warner, W. L., & Lunt, P. S. (1941). *The social life of a modern community*. New Haven: Yale University Press.
Warner, W. L., & Lunt, P. S. (1942). *The status system of a modern community*. New Haven: Yale University Press.
Warner, W. L., & Srole, L. (1945). *The social systems of American ethnic groups*. New Haven: Yale University Press.
Warner, S., & Wittner, J. (Eds.). (1998). *Gatherings in diaspora: Religious communities and the new immigration*. Philadelphia: Temple University Press.
Waugh, E. H., Abu-Laban, B., & Quereshi, R. (Eds.). (1983). *The Muslim community in North America*. Edmonton: The University of Alberta Press.
Weller, P. (Ed.). (1994). *Religions in the UK: A multi-faith directory*. Derby: University of Derby and Inter-Faith Network for the UK.
Williams, R. (1988). *Religions of immigrants from India and Pakistan: New threads in the American tapestry*. Cambridge: Cambridge University Press.
Wolf, R. C. (1947). *The Americanization of the German Lutherans 1638–1829*. Unpublished PhD Thesis, Yale University.
Woodson, C. G. (1921). *The history of the Negro church*. Washington, D.C.: The Associated Publishers.
Yang, F. (1998). Chinese conversion to evangelical Christianity: The importance of social and cultural contexts. *Sociology of Religion, 59*(3), 237–257.
Yang, F. (1999). *Chinese Christians in America: Conversion, assimilation and adhesive identities*. Pennsylvania: Pennsylvania University Press.
Yang, F., & Ebaugh, H. R. (2001a). Religion and ethnicity: The impact of majority/minority status in the home and host countries. *Journal for the Scientific Study of Religion, 40*(3), 367–378.
Yang, F., & Ebaugh, H. R. (2001b). Transformations in new immigrant religions and their global implications. *American Sociological Review, 66*, 269–288.
Yu, E.-Y. (1988). The growth of Korean Buddhism in the United States, with special reference to Southern California. *The Pacific World: Journal of the Institute of Buddhist Studies* n.s. 4 (Fall), 82–93.

Open Access This chapter is licensed under the terms of the Creative Commons Attribution 4.0 International License (http://creativecommons.org/licenses/by/4.0/), which permits use, sharing, adaptation, distribution and reproduction in any medium or format, as long as you give appropriate credit to the original author(s) and the source, provide a link to the Creative Commons license and indicate if changes were made.

The images or other third party material in this chapter are included in the chapter's Creative Commons license, unless indicated otherwise in a credit line to the material. If material is not included in the chapter's Creative Commons license and your intended use is not permitted by statutory regulation or exceeds the permitted use, you will need to obtain permission directly from the copyright holder.

Part II
The New Home

> *It may be argued that the past is a country from which we have all emigrated, that its loss is part of our common humanity. Which seems to be self-evidently true; but I suggest that the writer who is out-of-country and even out-of-language may experience this loss in an intensified form. It is made more concrete for him by the physical fact of discontinuity, of his present being in a different place from his past, of his being 'elsewhere'...human beings do not perceive things whole; we are not gods but wounded creatures, cracked lenses, capably only of fractured perceptions. Partial beings, in all the senses of that phrase. Meaning is a shaky edifice we build out of scraps, dogmas, childhood injuries, newspaper articles, chance remarks, old films, small victories, people hated, people loved; perhaps it is because of our sense of what is the case is constructed from such inadequate materials that we defend it so fiercely, even to the death.*
> Novelist Salman Rushdie
> *Imaginary Homelands* (1991: 12)

Salman Rushdie's words serve as a healthy reminder of how difficult it is to address people's lives and how much is lost when experiences are described as being the result of a few processes. Indubitably, we need to reduce the complexities of lives to be able to build general knowledge, yet we also need to insist on the acknowledgement of the complexity of people's experience and that none of us understand ourselves fully; indeed, verbalised experiences are in themselves rationalised narratives that order and photoshop our 'fractured perceptions'. By emphasising the concerns and strivings of migrants in what follows, we aim to consider the many different forms of actions – power practices – in relation to religions and religious living.

To be able to address the complex changes in the lives of migrants, we need to introduce some tools. French philosopher and theologian Michel de Certeau (1984: 37) separates between 'tactics' – which, as ways to take temporary control of situations when you are not in formal control, he considers the art of the weak – and 'strategies', which belong to influential agents. At the heart of the observation is the importance of power practices – and not only governments exercise strategic power; so do local agents who might have the ability to exercise control, while even the 'weak' exercise tactical power by resisting strategies or complying with them.

de Certeau further separates between 'place', an area as it is planned and set up, and 'space', the social practice of place. Thus, you make space in a place, often temporarily: for example, believers turn a street into a processional space when celebrating the passion of Christ or the martyrdom of Hussein, but once they are done, it is a regular street again. de Certeau's dichotomies should not be mistaken for absolute positions; they are, rather, tools of perception. This part will make use of the separations between strategies and tactics and place and space in order to identify some of the main processes in establishing, maintaining and developing religious communities in relation to migration.

Religious life in long-term or permanent international migration will eventually lead to space making and, not least, the construction of physical centres for religious practices. But space will also be made through public rituals and bodily practices. This space making may be social, political, economic, psychological and, of course, religious, although these categories overlap and our division is purely for presentational purposes. Space making is *social* in the sense that migrants are accompanied by a semiotic visibility, audibility and bodily presence (often with a gendered dimension), implying that the 'the outsiders' generate changes in society for 'the established' to use Norbert Elias and John L. Scotson's (1994) terminology. Elias and Scotson found that a social conflict they were studying mainly pitted the established and the outsiders against each other. We use the term 'the established' as we think that being established (or not) is just as important as being part of an imagined majority (or not) and, moreover, it includes already established minorities. Most European countries have well-established ethnic, religious or other minorities and it is well attested that new arrivals must negotiate social space with all those who are thus established, not merely the majority population.

Further, space making is *political* in the sense that creating documentation, such as residence or building permits, and registering religious organisations invoke the governance of a society. These actions involve political activities aimed at gaining special legal rights or exemptions, or even the right not to be discriminated against. Space making is *economic* in the sense that migrants receive support, pay taxes and make investments, while religious organisations are complex economic institutions potentially receiving large donations, paying salaries and taxes (or may be exempt from the latter if acknowledged) and/or receiving transnational or international support from governments. For example, the Moroccan and Turkish governments actively support diaspora citizens in their religious activities abroad (e.g., Nielsen & Otterbeck, 2016) and religious movements such as West African neo-Pentecostal movements and US-based Pentecostal groups back the mission in Europe (e.g., Pass, 2015). Space making is *psychological* in the sense that being able to make space is important for self-esteem, nurturing indigenousness, constituting a community as diasporic and feeling secure: becoming established, in other words. As space making is experienced as challenging by many – the established and newcomers (rather than outsiders) alike – this tends to take time and be expressed in symbolic actions, both tactical and strategic, which are met with support, resistance or, of course, indifference.

Finally, space making is *religious* in the sense that sooner or later elements of religions and religiosity become manifest when migrants show religious preferences in their quotidian rituals in public as well as in private, not least through a ritualisation of the body visible in clothing, bodily adornments (tattoos, jewellery) or food preferences, displayed in signs in stores announcing they sell halal or kosher products, or restaurants claiming they follow Vedic diet prescriptions. Temples, halls, churches, mosques, synagogues, yeshivas, dojos, gurdwaras and jamatkhanas change the face of cities. The cityscapes (think landscape) change with the initiatives of religious migrants.

References

de Certeau, M. (1984). *The practice of everyday life*. Berkeley: University of California Press.
Elias, N., & Scotson, J. L. (1994). *The established and the outsiders*. London: Sage.
Nielsen, J. S., & Otterbeck, J. (2016). *Muslims in western Europe* (4th ed.). Edinburgh University Press.
Pass, S. (2015). Mission from anywhere to Europe: Americans, Africans, and Australians coming to Amsterdam. *Mission Studies, 32*(1), 4–31.
Rushdie, S. (1991). *Imaginary homelands, 1981–1991*. London: Granta.

Chapter 3
Finding Tactics and Making Space: The Individuals and the Communities

In this chapter, we focus on international migration from the perspective of the migrants themselves, examining the different tactics and ways of space making they deploy. We begin with the religious lives of individual migrants, first providing a theoretical presentation of how religion can be understood as an individual yet social phenomenon. Migration changes the social structures of a person's life in many ways and, as a social phenomenon, religion is likely to go through similar drastic changes in connection with migration. Consequently, we need to know more about religion as a social structure and the function of it. Then we demonstrate how migrants' religious lives can be understood by addressing the issue of religious practices, how people's religion relates to integration and, finally, how religious beliefs may be a motivating factor in developing active citizenship.

We continue by describing and discussing the religious communities of which migrants may be part, illustrating the patterns of establishment of religious organisations, processes of community space making and how migrant communities relate to established religious organisations. We then relate these two perspectives – the individual and the more collective (the communities) – to transnational, global and technological contexts, which have changed immensely during the second half of the twentieth century and have had a deep impact on the migrants' religious lives (national context is the subject of Chap. 4). Chapter Three concludes with an in-depth presentation of how religious services are affected by migration, showing the close inter-relationship between the individual and the communities in terms of power practices in this area.

3.1 The Social Functions of Religion

3.1.1 Demographics

Demographic tendencies affect the process of shaping religious communities in new home countries. International migration to Europe tends to be imbalanced as to age and sex, especially labour migration. Many migrants are young, sometimes only children, and migration from many places tends to be dominated by one sex – often, but not always, men – but if migration continues over time, this balance tends to level out. For example, the 1960s labour migration from Anatolian Turkey to Sweden was dominated by young men but this changed during the 1970s when women, children and some older cohorts started to arrive. Soon the group consisted of roughly equal numbers of men and women. Refugees arriving in Europe are also primarily young; as many as 25 percent (2015) and 34 percent (2016) were children according to UNHCR data on refugees arriving to EU by sea. Male refugees are at least twice as common, some years three times as common as female.

People of the same faith are inclined to create communities which then provide and uphold moral regulations to demarcate inclusion and exclusion. Some are based on religious dogmas, others on general, regionally shared morality at times legitimated by reference to religion. A rule of thumb is that the more rural and collectively oriented a society, the more tightly knit the relations between morals, culture and religion, while the more urban and highly educated the group, the more likely religion is experienced as demarcated in time and space, and associated with theology and the performance of rituals. However, such a general rule is problematic in relation to mega-cities like Istanbul, Teheran or Lagos, where whole areas may be rural in character due to rapid urbanisation and the expansion of the city's boundaries. The interlacing of perceptions of morals, culture and religion should not be presupposed, but researched.

3.1.2 Religion as a Social Structure

Peter Berger and Thomas Luckmann (1966) made visible the social structures that support the relevance of, for example, religious practices and socio-religious norms, and labelled them plausibility structures. Values and norms are continually and unreflectively perpetuated in families, schools, religious institutions, media and so on, and tend to be taken for granted when growing up surrounded by social structures that are fairly in tune with each other. After migration, plausibility structures are generally challenged by changed social structures in the new place of residence. The lack of some, or all, former plausibility structures, are challenged by, new, social structures built on other values and norms.

When individuals, families or groups migrate from one place to another and then form interacting social groups in a new country, differences in norms and moral expectations between the established population of the new country and the migrant group tend to stand out more than similarities. Social structures and norms in the new country are upheld and reproduced by wide-reaching public institutions, such as schools, health services and government institutions, as well as workplaces and associations for leisure activities. In contrast, many migrant religious communities strive to offer plausibility structures that uphold unchanged or revitalised religious values and moral expectations, but without the structure of former milieus and the complex of practices and institutions to support or enforce worldviews. Exposure to competing social structures is known to give rise to the risk of individual cognitive dissonance as well as tensions between spouses, between generations in families, and between people of, nominally, the same religious background but with different practices and norms, aspiring to different lives (e.g., Blaschke, 2000; Roy, 2004); it also affects relations with the established population, their expectations and preconceived notions of people and the position of religion in society (e.g., Nielsen & Otterbeck, 2016).

Migrants have a statistical tendency to settle where others of similar background live, thereby maintaining some control and benefiting from contacts and solidarity and marking big cities like London with its migration history. Chinatown is positioned at the centre; the East End was long the home of the largest Jewish population, replaced from the 1960s by Bangladeshi migrants who took up residency as the Jewish population relocated to parts of North London like Stamford Hill and Golders Green. Other areas, like Wood Green, are dominated by or at least have a clear presence of Kurdish, Polish and West Indian migrants, with flourishing restaurants, grocery stores and religious centres catering for specific ethno-religious groups and making up a home away from home. Throughout history, such settlement patterns for migrants and ethnic minorities have grown organically but have also, at times, been ordered by the authorities, the Jewish Ghetto in Rome being the prime symbolic example of the latter.

3.1.3 *Morals and the Bracketing of Them*

Exposure to a variety of plausibility structures associated with different groups is not necessarily a problem. People have a remarkable capacity to manage concurrently belonging to several such structures, upholding different values that shape so-called 'moral registers' which the individual can navigate. The theory of moral registers has been developed by Samuli Schielke (2015) in his study of young men in a large village just outside Alexandria, Egypt, where he stresses 'the performative, situational, and dialogic character of norms' (p. 54). Schielke describes some parallel moral registers of particular relevance for his informants, among them religion, social respect, family solidarity and being seen as individually of good character (a good friend, a good son). By definition, registers are competences that can be mobilised. While not to be taken lightly, registers do not control individuals; rather, the knowledge of the norms implied by a register may make you calculate that you should abide by the ideal to be perceived as respectable and acceptable, both in your own and in others' eyes. In the context Schielke analyses, Islam takes on an overarching function but can tactically be bracketed when having a love affair or when horsing around with friends; thus, Islamic morals are discursively affirmed but not necessarily honoured in practice. The content and function of religious morals is a matter of empirical enquiry but the existence of overlapping morals registers can be assumed. Thus, while the young men's plausibility structures homogenously support the importance of religion, as individuals they are also, in specific situations, part of other plausibility structures that support other moral registers.

In Otterbeck's (2010a, 2015) research on young adults with a Muslim background in two cities in southern Scandinavia, there is a clear gender dimension to the bracketing of religious morals. The young adult men who upheld moral rules at home – not only to please parents but because it felt right and part of their religion and ethnic authenticity – sometimes ate non-halal meat, sampled alcohol and had romantic relations when out of home's reach. The young adult women did not admit to any such transgressions, but they were aware of such transgressions and torn between pride in being mature and consistent in their behaviour and irritated by the laxness of others, as it challenged the meaningfulness of their own abiding by the norms. Yet none of the women wore a veil (apart from in prayer) or were equally attached to an Islamic worldview as their parents. They were in flux. As young as they were, in their late teens, they could already reflect on the different phases of religious practice they had traversed, and their changed perceptions of what Islam meant, and they assumed and discussed future changes.

Ambivalence about belonging and alienation in relation to possible past, present and future identifications among migrants is not uncommon (e.g., Magnusson, 2011; Nordin, 2004). As illustrated by the Rushdie quote above, and as pointed out by Peter Kivisto (2014: 35), memoirs, novels and movies by migrants frequently revolve around ambivalence about belonging, and identification with elements including religious truths and structures. Sometimes, researchers frame this as taking on multiple identities, thus underlining the different roles one might play in different and separate social contexts, such as home and the workplace. Many contexts are, however, interlaced; it is up to the researcher to find out how. For example, it is fully possibly for a football club to be intimately tied to an ethno-religious community with a migration history, making identities like player/supporter and devotee/member coincide (e.g., Aktan, 2017; Müller, 2014).

3.1.4 Gender, Social Norms, and Integration

One important and pervasive function of religion as social structure is to do with gender. One can even claim that all religions construct gender in different ways, usually involving the subordination of women (e.g., Khan, 2021). For example, religious social norms have a long history of being gendered, in local or regional religious traditions as well as in intellectual interpretations. When migrating to a new society, gendered mobility becomes important for the type of integration performed.

Therefore, we must ask ourselves questions about whether the migrant will be seen as turning against religious norms if marrying outside their natal religious group, or not. For some like the Druze there is a strong tradition of endogamy for both men and women. A Druze risks excommunication if breaking these rules. Muslim women may similarly have to adhere to endogamy, risking social exclusion if they do not, while Muslim men, according to common theology, can marry a believing woman outside Islam, and marry even non-believing women in practice. Still, in Europe there is growing pressure on Islamic leaders to accept marriages between Muslim women and non-Muslim men and of same-sex couples (e.g., Petersen, 2020). Increasingly, Jews marry non-Jews in Europe despite theological concerns about this. But, as Dencik (2009) demonstrates, marriage between a Jewish man and a non-Jewish woman is more acceptable than the other way around. Thus, a classical measure of integration, as noted by Gordon as early as 1964 – intermarriage between a migrant group and the established population over the generations – will be affected by how people experience the degree of freedom or guidance provided by religious norms and possible group pressures, and is, therefore, not only about general integration. What is considered plausible, suitable, shameful or unacceptable through a religious lens varies with gender and religious belonging, but also with the generations over time. Thus, religious norms, ideas and group belonging are potential factors in how migrants form attachments and interests.

Practicing *gendered* religious morals, rituals and habits is particularly complex when the established consider – or when opinion makers try to influence others to consider – the practices problematic or even provocative of political and social turbulence; these have also become crucial ammunition for populist, nationalist and racist politicians, as is evident in discussions about Muslim veils, Sikh turbans or reservations about shaking hands.

Thus, researchers must take religious traditions and gender into account when discussing general integration if they are to reach a better understanding of groups that might not fit into overall models.

3.2 The Migrant's Religious Life and Its Effects

When studying how individual migrants select tactics and make space in their religious lives, the great variation in ways of relating to religious norms and rituals and their dependence on every conceivable element in the migration processes becomes apparent. Ethnographic and micro-sociological methods are the most likely way to capture such complexities.

To illustrate that religion can really be a very crucial part of life and not only a leisure time activity, we first address two fields of ritualisation: everyday ritual behaviour and life-cycle rituals. Then we examine a well-established discussion about religion as a resource or a hindrance to becoming part of a society. To complement this, we also discuss how religion can be an important part of what motivates active citizenship.

3.2.1 Ritualisation and Quotidian Rituals

Ritualisation is the process of making something into a ritual, but also the appropriation of prior ritualisations existing within a religion, and investigating it is good strategy when both illustrating and discussing religious life. Some rituals are quotidian—that is, ritual behaviour brought into the everyday life—while others are regular routines (for example weekly prayers) or calendrical and lifecycle rituals (Knott, 2016). We consciously use the word ritual in regard to quotidian activities to stress how physical practices like clothing, movement, emotions, eating and drinking can be ritualised, that is, ordered by theology and tradition, and then embodied. Practiced quotidian rituals signal complex and situation-bound webs of morals, group belonging and gender roles (quite often relating to modesty), and enable others to interpret the level and type of religion of practicing people, which of course includes the risk of misinterpretation.

In a diaspora situation, migrants will find some rituals more important than others and probably make a selection. Unlike quotidian rituals, some are profoundly associated with a sacred geography left behind, such as visits to shrines, temples and saints' tombs, the prayers said there and the expected spiritual rewards for the visit. Yet other rituals may be upheld, partly maintained or re-ritualised and re-contextualised. After migration, many regular ritual routines and calendrical rituals may instead take place in the private sphere of families, with the specific problem that these holidays might fall on general workdays. Some may prefer to pray several times daily, which can become problematic in the new setting. While European countries generally protect individual freedom of religion, people of minority religions generally have no specific state-guaranteed right to ask for extra days off each year to celebrate calendric religious feasts, although many workplaces today understand the need for short vacations on such occasions, making them fairly easy to celebrate.

When quotidian rituals among migrants, and others, are brought to school, to work and out in public, by default these make space. Sometimes, the possibility of practicing quotidian rituals depends on the cooperation and goodwill of the more established population. Will the army and school serve halal and kosher food? Will employers accept Sikh turbans, Muslim veils, Jewish shtreimels and other visible religious symbols? Will a prayer room be available? Will avoiding alcohol at a workplace party be accepted, barely tolerated or seen as anti-social? Can migrants initiate change by pointing out their need to engage in a practice that differs from those of the established groups? Because of the difficulties in maintaining quotidian rituals, some migrants privatise these practices, for example, by using the headscarf only when praying, eating kosher and halal primarily at home, or shaking hands across assumed gender boundaries at work with colleagues and customers but never in contexts controlled by religious peers. Such tactical compartmentalisations of everyday life may be crucial techniques for coping with social and religious expectations (remember moral registers) in new contexts (e.g., Jouili, 2015; Otterbeck, 2010a).

Others insist on practicing quotidian rituals at work and school or argue for the right to do so. This has led to pragmatic solutions and integration, but also to legal discussions and legal cases both on national and EU levels. The outcomes have varied a lot depending on country, but also on when during the last decades the discussions or cases have taken place (e.g., Jakku, 2018). We return to the state-level politics of religion in Chap. 4.

3.2.2 *Ritualisation and Lifecycle Rituals*

The interconnectedness of private, shared and public space is well illustrated in lifecycle rituals, such as those related to birth, marriage and death. In her PhD thesis (2001), Nathal Dessing interviews Muslim practitioners about lifecycle rituals (related to birth, adulthood, marriage and death) and observes their enactment, both as they are performed in the Netherlands and as they were (and are) performed in their country of origin. Dessin concludes that many of these rituals have changed in various ways in the Netherlands, some have kept their original form and others have disappeared. The reasons for the changes or disappearance, Dessing argues, are heavily dependent on the new setting. The Muslims studied strive to retain the rituals as before but often must adapt or abandon them due to their new social, cultural and juridical circumstances. A distinctive tendency in the processes of adaptation of the rituals is attrition, that is, the lifecycle rituals become fewer and less varied. This has, for example, to do with a loss of competence over time among practitioners, the reduction in the number of people upholding them where they live, educational levels and institutional resources (Dessing, 2001, see also Holm Pedersen, 2009; Andizian, 1986).

Another aspect that tends to follow from migration is the theologisation of religion which occurs when local traditions, sometimes experienced as being at the centre of a broader religion, are challenged by migration. The generation growing up in the new home country sometimes fails to see the relevance of rituals connected to regional cults, a specific religious geography or flow of life; rather, the rituals at the core of normative theology are those that are perceived as relevant (e.g., Otterbeck, 2010a; Waardenburg, 1978).

Such changes in lifecycle rituals are obviously not unique to Muslim immigrants. Anne Sigfrid Grønseth's (2018) research on Tamil Hindus in Norway shows similar patterns. In a case study of the funeral of a Tamil refugee who suffered a fatal, work-related accident in Northern Norway, Grønseth demonstrates how the mourning Tamil community 'carefully considered appropriate funerary practices, values and needs amid calculations of the risk of exposing what could be regarded as their "exotic Tamilness'" (p. 2617), thereby risking increased marginalisation in relation to the established social structures. In the end, the funeral – taking place in a Protestant church, the service held by a Catholic priest, but including Hindu practices – rather encouraged cohesion. In the shared human experience of loss, grief and consolation, integration between Tamils and Norwegian co-workers was made possible (see also Fesenmyer, 2017; Fibiger, 2017; Hämmerli & Mucha, 2014; Fog Olwig, 2009).

3.2.3 Religion as a Resource or Hindrance for Integration

It has been pointed out in migration research that religion, or religiosity, constitutes a facilitator for integration into the USA, but has other functions in Europe (e.g., Foner & Alba, 2008). While the argument has some substantial merit, it is too crude. Instead, we need to ask: when does religion facilitate integration? Well, firstly it can do so by strengthening the individual, being something in which to place trust that provides answers to existential questions, such as those related to the migration process the person is undergoing. Other answers are likely to be when religion provides social capital in the form of networks that can be helpful when seeking opportunities (housing, work, partners) and as cultural capital (knowledge and sought-after competence, including in religious fields). Charles Hirschman (2004) suggests that religion, for migrants, is a way to gain refuge, respectability and resources, and thus can facilitate integration. We also need to investigate when religion forms a hindrance. Religion does not help integration when stereotypes, dislike or hatred on the part of the established or other out-group migrants stigmatize, discriminate or physically threaten. It neither helps when religious rules and norms hinder social, economic and professional life, and when loyalties to different identities clash in bothersome ways.

Thus, religion can function as both 'adaptive solidarity', which indicates processes in which religion is highlighted and strengthened as a way to facilitate integration into the larger society, and as 'defensive solidarity', which implies processes in which religion is highlighted and strengthened as protection against perceived threats and exclusion from established social structures (e.g., Breton, 2012).

One of the reasons that researchers have concluded that religious engagement is good for integration in the USA is that congregations function to a high degree as networks for work and other opportunities (e.g., Chen, 2006; Hirschman, 2004; Lorentzen et al., 2009). Because of the expectations this raises among migrants, some find themselves engaging, regardless of personal religious (dis)interest, and some may even convert to locally established groups as, generally, people of all faiths care for converts (Kivisto, 2014: Chap. 2). However, in a study of Chinese migrants to the Greater Washington DC area, Yang (1998) cautions against monocausal explanations about conversion reasons and finds that other factors, such as the trajectory of religion in communist China, clearly affect the wish to explore Christianity. Further, in some environments, like college campuses, evangelical

Christians, as well as some Muslims groups, are well organised and active in proselytising.

In European countries, by comparison, religion tends to have another function. Service attendance in many European countries is generally low, meaning that parish life has to a lesser degree provided the social networks and solidarity needed for finding work or housing (e.g., Bruce, 2002); however, within certain regions or cities, it might be as important as in the USA, while religious organisations set up by migrants have at times proven to be efficient social networks leading to economic integration. Some groups, especially revivalist groups and those who may have already been ethno-religious minorities in the country of origin, tend to show strong solidarity with fellow believers, thus bettering the chances of the individual engaging with or belonging to them. Such solidarity may also be shown because of shared language or national background. For example, when Tatar Muslim immigrant Ali Zakerov fled to Stockholm in the 1940s, he went to the Jewish furrier Harry Rock and appealed to the latter's sense of solidarity as they both spoke Yiddish, which Zakerov had picked up from Jewish friends in Tallinn. He then worked for Jewish furriers until retirement. In the late 1940s, together with a few friends, Zakerov founded the first Islamic organisation in Sweden and served as its first chairman (Sorgenfrei, 2020).

Thus, while not arguing that everyone has an instrumental attitude to religious organisations, we may conclude that at least some strive to find socio-economic benefits as well as religious comfort by engaging with religious organisations. The chances of gaining from social capital in relation to religious environments seem better in the USA than in most European countries, as mentioned; still, the intersection between religious organisations, economic integration and migration in different European contexts merits more research. As a suggestion, researchers would do well to survey rural and small city milieus and a variety of different religious groups.

Yet another aspect of integration comes into view from the social psychological perspective explored by Lars Dencik (1993), who argues that Jews in Sweden have the potential benefit of bifocal vision: one set trained by the Swedish experience and one by the Jewish. This would also cover religious literacy in both Christianity and Judaism. Yet instead of unequivocally postulating this as an advantage, he also points out the risks of not managing to code switch or learn from experience, although successfully negotiating these pitfalls and knowing more than one context intimately no doubt has potential advantages. The ability to code switch and double competences or the lack thereof are interesting research areas when approaching migrants.

Above we mentioned discrimination and stereotypes. Harsh, discriminatory opinions and acts directed towards a religious other are, sadly, found all through human history and are not unique to contemporary times, nor to Europe and North America, although the target changes. While anti-Catholic sentiments have somewhat diminished in Protestant environments in Europe and North America compared to the beginning of the twentieth century, anti-Muslim sentiments have soared. Outbreaks and new trajectories of antisemitism are ever-present while anti-Buddhism is marginal (we return to this in Sect. 4.3). However, in addition to creating fear and victims of violence, ruining opportunities and disrupting integration of all sorts, discrimination can also cause people to mobilise, to speak up and engage when opportunities arise. It is to such engagement we now turn.

3.2.4 Religion and Active Citizenship

For some immigrants, religion is a motivational factor in developing active citizenship. Engaging in charities, NGOs or political parties – locally or nationally – may be motivated by religious ethics and belonging. All major religious traditions have welfare elements of which healthcare, education and socio-economic welfare are generally key (for more on charity see Sect. 5.5). Economic remittances sent from individual migrants to family, relatives and aid organisations in former home countries are on a scale vastly outperforming the aid programs of European states (e.g., Kapur & McHale, 2009). Besides being a decent thing to do, religious rewards, obligations and motivations play crucial roles in this, a welfare tradition that often also covers supporting local religious organisations and religious specialists.

Interesting patterns emerge when examining activities in the new home country. It is well established in the study of immigrants within political science that it is more likely for the political energy of immigrants to be directed towards NGOs and unions, rather than being channelled through established political parties (e.g., Stoltz, 2000). This likely holds true for migrants with a religious background who may engage socially and politically through religious organisations as well, particularly charities working for the betterment of the lives of fellow believers (and at times more broadly than that). Jewish, Muslim, Sikh, Christian, Buddhist, Hindu and Druze charity funds, among others, operate all over Europe, becoming part of the expected normality of cities through their space making (see Sect. 5.5).

Other migrants – either motivated by or working against religious morals – engage in national politics. Exemplifying the latter is the world renown, self-identifying ex-Muslim, Ayaan Hirsi Ali, who has a Somali background and has used her knowledge about migrant contexts and Islam to create a political career in the Netherlands at a time when the political discourse on Islam and Muslim migrants is changing from one favouring accommodation to criticism (e.g., Buruma, 2006). Typically, when migrant politicians with a minority religious background engage in politics, they tend, at least initially, to profile themselves as experts on migrants, partly because it is expected of them but also due to engagement and competence (e.g., Cato & Otterbeck, 2014). It becomes clear when studying individual politicians with migrant backgrounds and strong attachments to a minority faith that their loyalty is often questioned; they may be regarded as 'Uncle Toms' or suspected of double agendas due to their engagement in multiple spheres. It is, moreover, hard to reconcile national discourses with those prevalent in religious migrants' circles, which are quite often in different languages with different rhetorical traditions (e.g., Cato & Otterbeck, 2014; Jakku, 2018; Petersen, 2020).

3.3 The Establishment of Religious Organisations

Typically, most migrants to Europe since WWII have arrived either as low-skilled workers or as refugees. There is no shortage of highly skilled migrants, students, businesspeople and other professionals, but statistically they make up a minority. Thus, when establishing new religious organisations, the restricted financial resources of members has often decided where to rent or build a room for services and administration. As many migrants have taken up residency in social housing blocks encircling European cities, this is also where mosques, temples, churches and other religious organisations' buildings are to be found. As we shall see in the next section, the dynamics are a bit different for transnational and global movements.

Two kinds of migrant organisations tend to engage in religion: cultural associations engaging in religion on holidays or at ritualised moments, like holding a prayer to bless food, and religion-centred communities. While the first type is often created by enthusiasts wanting to keep the complexities of their culture alive, at least in one space, the second type is, unsurprisingly, started by people who experience their religion as special and crucial in ways that sometimes intimidate those less passionate, who might want to engage with religion from a more cultural or less serious perspective. In real life the two organisation types often overlap, especially for ethno-religious groups like Sikhs, Jews, Yazidis, Alevis and Syriac Orthodox Christians. Still, we find it important to stress the two types as quite a number of organisations are characterised by exactly this difference.

3.3.1 The Patterns of Establishment

Drawn from a range of observations, the following tends to be the pattern for the establishment of religious organisations (e.g., Rogers, 2019; Mack, 2017; Jacobsen & Myrvold, 2011; Maussen, 2007; Waardenburg, 1983). The first migrants of a denomination will worship at home. The next step is to join forces with peers and seek temporary, rented facilities, religious or profane, often on the outskirts of towns, in social housing or industrial areas. Religious representatives, at this stage of the process, often travel around and hold ceremonies in various parts of a country or a region. Here Christian migrant groups have had an advantage in societies with established Christian denominations, as it has been easier to access, rent or borrow more centrally located places of worship or simply exercise religious practices as part of religious ceremonies already taking place. For example, the studies in Goodhew and Cooper (2019) demonstrate how some Christian groups have managed to find central locations, perhaps sharing or temporarily renting spaces in mega-cities like London. Yet racism and adverse expectations can hinder smooth integration into existing religious structures, as experienced by the so called Windrush generation – migrants from the Caribbean who primarily arrived in the UK during the 1950s and 1960s. Even though most Windrush-generation migrants could find their Christian direction in the UK, the urge to form their own congregations became acute as they simply did not feel welcome in the community (see further discussion in Sect. 3.5).

The tactics of making space for religion can be illustrated by 'guest workers' in France during the 1970s, who often lived in *foyers*[1] in which there were no rooms for religious practice, although workers belonging to Christian faiths could celebrate their traditions outside the *foyers* – a facility not available to the Muslim workers at the time. This led to demands for the same opportunities among the Muslim workers, and in the mid-1970s they held strikes in order to get prayer rooms and ritually prepared food in the *foyers*. The companies responsible realised that it was necessary for them to accommodate these requirements, and in less than ten years, 80 percent of such housing in France had installed prayer rooms (Maussen, 2007: 992f).

The next step in the establishment pattern is to find a more long-term place, rented or not, often on the outskirts of towns where rents or building plots are affordable. In the final stage, a purpose-built structure is planned and possibly even built, preferably in a more central location; the last step is notoriously difficult to execute and numerous projects have failed over the years.

This process is well-illustrated by Jennifer Mack's (2017) study of Södertälje in Sweden, a small town with 75,000 inhabitants close to Stockholm. Here she demonstrates the importance of churches and buildings for religious celebrations to the Middle Eastern Christian immigrants in the town. Even though they have settled in a country in which their religion, on a general level, coincides with that of the established majority, there was a strong desire among them to have their own premises. To start with, at the end of the 1960s, they borrowed or rented churches from the Church of Sweden, but in 1981 the construction of a large, purpose-built church was initiated, inaugurated in 1983 as the first Syriac Orthodox church in Europe, with the capacity for almost 1000 worshippers. The architect hired was not familiar with Syriac Orthodox traditions, and from the outside there were few signs it was a church, so, two years later, the congregation applied for a permit to build a bell tower, only to be used during the daytime, giving rise to numerous negative public reactions resembling the protests against the construction of minarets in Europe. Yet the bell tower was realised and, further, the first church that they had borrowed was also bought by the Syriac Orthodox congregation. Today the elderly in the congregation mostly use this one because it is situated close to where they live, whereas the newer church is situated further away. In 2020, almost forty years after the inauguration of their first purpose-built church, the Syriac Orthodox Church in Södertälje owns four – two purpose-built and two reconstructed – and we find, in total, thirteen purpose-built and about fifteen reconstructed Syriac Orthodox churches in Sweden.

Another way of establishing space for religious collective practices is the common phenomenon of 'the pop-up mosque', a term coined by Petersen (2020) to capture how enthusiasts temporarily turn whatever facility is available into a mosque

---

[1] Cheap housing in French cities, originally meant for temporary residence.

space, transporting the transformative materiality of the 'mosque' in bags. In this context, the notion of 'mosque' refers more to an idea of a community than an actual building and is well worth exploring in relation to religions other than Islam. The formation of 'pop-up religious spaces' is typical of enthusiastic groups with lots of drive but few resources, not least new, liberally minded associations (for example LBGTQIA+ groups), youth organisations and newly arrived migrants committed to celebrating an important holiday together.

A common scenario in the initial phase of the establishment of religious organisations is that of a few passionate enthusiasts spending substantial amounts of time and money planning, administrating and searching for funding, thus performing an important service for the community. However, if they are successful, few let go and they remain entrenched in the hierarchy. In the long run this may not be ideal as organisations need to develop, meet new challenges and handle generation shifts. Another risk, or possibility, is that the organisation – if successful – will be targeted for 'hostile takeover' by economically or socially stronger groups, a sponsor or by groups of a different theological leaning. Therefore, when migrants are building religious structures and making space, researchers need to investigate the politics of the groups in question to understand change, motives and individual and group tactics in the ongoing struggle for control over resources and institutions.

3.3.2 *The Processes of Space Making and the Emotions Involved*

Making space for the presence of religious organisations, buildings and manifestations – visually and audibly – invites emotions: feelings of pride, authenticity, rootedness, achievement, nostalgia, sacredness and possibly boredom, angst, forced compliance and alienation, making them interesting places to study.

Frequently, religious organisations are rather invisible in their initial phases, typically consisting of the name of an organisation by a doorbell in a suburb or industrial area; however, as being visible and being accepted are closely related, many strive for wider recognition. One way is through space making. Religious organisations may book public places or ask permission for a procession and, if successful, may gain recognition for this. In London in the 2020s, most people know when it is Diwali (the festival of light in November), as the Hindu festival is celebrated with spectacular fireworks. Some parks are turned into Hindu festival areas blaring bhangra music classics. Similarly, 'Eid in the Square' is a yearly Muslim celebration in Trafalgar Square, London, taking place the first Saturday after Id al-fitr. On the surface, it is yet another celebration, with music, food stands and crowds, but, if attentive, a visitor will find Muslim charity organisations and books on Islam, and may note that among the musical acts are Qawwali artists playing pieces from the famous Pakistani Sufi music genre. The important thing is that both celebrations make space or, more precisely, allow the religious groups to define space on their own terms, albeit temporarily.

It is easier to make space when supported by the likeminded. Thus, many new migrants turn to religious organisations already established by migrants from their own faith, ethnic or language group for initial support. It is likely that this will come in different forms: economic aid, contacts, comfort, legal advice, emotional support and friendliness, in a situation that might not otherwise be supportive or patient enough with challenges such as language shortcomings. Through this, the religious organisation will become a home away from home.

For example, in a study of Egyptian, Iraqi and Assyrian Christians in Denmark, Sara Lei Sparre and Lise Paulsen Galal (2018) explicate how retaining religious practices helps these immigrants to come close to fellow immigrants and to a pre-migration 'homeland'. The religious services do not only serve as practices that bring them closer to God, but also function to bring members of the religious diaspora group closer together and to reconnect them with the 'homeland'. Since very few of the congregations have their own church buildings, they must adapt to shape this sense of 'homeland'. To celebrate liturgy in these borrowed churches, the community needs to transform a Protestant setting into an Eastern Orthodox, using methods like the pop-up mosques mentioned above. There is a lot of effort put into this but also into fundraising and planning to build or buy churches of their own that resemble those from the homeland as much as possible. This reflects the process of shaping 'a sensory bombardment of sounds, smells and sights' (p.11), as 'the church space has the power to awaken a sensorial experience' (p. 11) of attending a church in the former homeland. Through this, participants in the rituals can attend church services as if they were in their former homelands, meaning that they can be in both the new homeland and the former one simultaneously (Sparre & Galal Paulsen, 2018).

While the migrant generations seek to recreate familiar space that reflects the former homeland, a younger generation growing up in the new country might perceive this differently; indeed, Otterbeck (2010a, 2015) found that the nostalgia of the migrant generations was counterproductive in attracting youth. For example, the aesthetics, the archaic language in preaching and the insistence on gender segregation rather hindered participation. Instead, it was other activities like Qur'an schools, open discussions and playing football in the mosque grounds that appealed.

When religious organisations take form in the new country, they do so in state territories with specific laws and bureaucratic traditions. We devote Chap. 4 to situations that occur in connection with that.

3.3.3 Support and Conflict

In Europe, many migrants, both Christian non-Christian, have experienced support offered by local churches or other established religious organisations. Numerous religious NGOs and organisations provide aid, services and emotional, legal and economic support to migrants, on an individual as well as organisational level (e.g., Straut-Eppsteiner & Hagan, 2016). This can take the form of already established charity work and assistance from interfaith groups, although many of the latter have only been initiated during the twenty-first century as a direct response to contemporary migration (for more on interfaith groups see Sect. 4.3.2.3 and, on charity, Sect. 5.5). An example from the Swedish context is the Muslim Swedish Ibn Rushd Study Association, which started as part of the educational association Sensus, one of the largest in Sweden and strongly anchored in Christian tradition. Sensus allowed Ibn Rushd to grow and consolidate itself and it now operates independently while retaining working relations with Sensus. The Muslim Scouts, the Syriac Orthodox Scouts and the Muslim sobriety movement of Sweden have similar tales to tell (Otterbeck, 2010b). Another example of cooperation from Sweden is the long-term assistance offered by the Jewish congregation in Malmö in male circumcisions among Muslims (Nordin & Schölin, 2011).

We are not familiar with any European research drawing theoretical conclusions from the above. Yet, based on North American research (e.g., Kivisto, 2014; Stepick et al., 2009), it is fair to assume that a lack of social capital is a barrier to becoming part of a new society – many people experience downward social mobility when migrating – and that positive and creative relations with already established citizens, organisations and fellow migrants are likely to be extremely valuable for language development, networking, job opportunities, help when contacting authorities and so on. It also gives both the established and the newcomers a chance to acquire first-hand knowledge about the cultural habits and conventions of the other.

Of course, not everyone is pleased. The physical presence of minority religions associated with migration also causes negative reaction in the established populations of Europe. Buildings seem to be obvious targets for hate crimes and those owned by religious organisations started by migrants are frequently vandalised or even torched in the cloak of darkness. This is especially true of mosques and synagogues, but at times the churches of Christian minorities also suffer the same fate.

Further, and not to be ignored, is that many conflicts have translocal manifestations. The tension between Sunni and Shia Muslims in the Middle East during the reign of the Islamic State was reflected in attacks against each other in European environments, while the sectarian aspects of the Syrian war were also duplicated in Europe. Meanwhile, the Israeli–Palestinian / Islam–Judaism tension increases anti-semitism and feeds Islamophobic voices, seen, for example, in how Christian minorities from the Middle East refuse to cooperate in interfaith groups if Muslims from the Middle East are part of the meetings. At times, different Muslim groups from different parts of the Middle East will not accept each other either (e.g., Nordin, 2017, see also Karner & Parker, 2008).

3.4 Transnational Spaces and Global Movements

Remarkable changes have taken place since WWII in the technological capacity to communicate and do business over long distances. Then it was possible, but expensive and difficult; now it is easy and affordable, even for many quite poor people in the Global South. The mobile telephone call to loved ones announcing the successful arrival of a migrant who has attempted a journey is a priority. Communication techniques have also affected the theorisation of migration and religion. Before the 1990s, international migration effectively meant that many long-distance migrants lost contact with former environments despite letters with photos sent and expensive phone calls made. People who travelled were tasked with the transfer of money, photographs, documents, gossip and news. Because of distances that were difficult to bridge, migration research in effect concentrated on the present context of the migrants and prioritised studying them as part of a new state.

Since the 1990s much has changed. Social media apps have increased the possibility of maintaining contact with family, relatives, friends and co-religionists. Until the global Covid-19 pandemic crisis that started 2020, mobility steadily increased and airfares kept being reduced. Travelling religious specialists could make short visits and migrants could visit larger religious festivities in former home countries (if not at odds with the government). Admittedly, the possibility of international travel was and is still conditioned by citizenship or lack thereof. Further, satellite TV channels and the ever-expanding usefulness of the internet have vastly facilitated access to religious information, founding texts, religious preachers and religious music and artists. This has made migration researchers more aware that transnational and translocal relations needed to be investigated, rethought and theorised. It also challenges and blurs the notion of divisions in power practices in space making between tactics or 'bottom-up actions', and strategies or 'top-down actions'.

3.4.1 *Transnational Spaces and Social Remittances*

According to Thomas Faist (2004), international migration research started to include transnational migration in the early 1990s, resulting in the development of sophisticated theories about it. One of the researchers to gain fame for her studies on transnational spaces and religion was US researcher Peggy Levitt (1998, 1999, 2001), who demonstrated just how intertwined migrants may remain with the social environment they have 'left'. She minted the concept 'social remittances' – which supplements the concept of 'economic remittances' – focusing on religious ideas, values, behaviour and practices that migrants, with or without intending to, pick up in a new country and remit to their former home environment. Levitt showed how religious change in the new country also affected religious ideas and practices among relatives and close friends in the country of origin. In other words, through letters, goods and also new techniques in communication, a sense of community was maintained that formed a 'transnational village'; thus, socialisation processes – those never-ending processes of becoming and remaining part of different social structures by gaining (often tacit) knowledge about normality – took on a new configuration for the community.

Otterbeck (2010a) gives examples of how teenage cousins growing up in different countries exchange stories about their sibling parents' ways of raising them, knowledge that can be used in future negotiations about what the teenagers should be allowed to do. In this case, it worked both ways, according to the interviewed teenagers living in Scandinavia – at times they experienced stricter rules than their cousins in their parents' former home countries. Another example of transnational social remittances, but on a more political level, is the Irrecha thanksgiving ritual among the Oromo group from Ethiopia. For various reasons it had lost significance somewhat in Ethiopia but started to be observed more regularly in the global diaspora, connecting it to the heartland heritage and empowering the ethno-religious group abroad; its reappearance in the diaspora also functioned to challenge and mobilise resistance to the political suppression of the group in Ethiopia (Regassa & Zeleke, 2014).

Thus, migration researchers should consider multi-layered contexts, applying, for example, network analysis to track people's social field(s). Pnina Werbner (2003) has studied a regional cult celebrating the Sufi Saint Zindapir (d. 1999) in north-western Pakistan and its ties, social structures and relations in, not least, Manchester and Birmingham, UK. Werbner concentrates on how 'Sufism is performative and embodied in ritual practice' (p. 29), demonstrated in the public religious processions the Sufi group arranged in Manchester. This space making in the new environment gained authenticity and prompted engagement in the form of blessings and objects sent from the centre of the regional cult. This in turn engendered continuous communication and travel, primarily by the appointed representatives of Zindapir, but UK migrants returning to Pakistan, sometimes with newly acquired wealth and status, also tied together the different regions in transnational relations. Further, followers experienced that Zindapir himself communicated through everyday miracles and dreams regardless of where they were; it is expected of Sufi sheikhs to be able to transcend time and space.

The transnational experience often involves either circular migration or setting up two homes. Emigrants may have the right to buy and own property in former home countries and many have dual (or more) citizenship, which helps, and local contacts who facilitate affairs. The dream of return among migrants, not least refugees, is kept alive by many. It is well-attested that Palestinians who left their homes when Israel was founded have held onto their front door keys (e.g., Sa'di & Abu-Lughud, 2007). In other cases, the connection is less concrete or is symbolised by an investment in property or the building (or maintenance) of religious buildings. Further, being buried in the village or city of origin is of great importance to many, even to those who otherwise lead lives little concerned with religion. Such dreams of return, expressed through what Bolognani and Erdal (2017) call 'return imaginaries', are a realistic alternative for some; for others they are not, due to numerous factors such as financial position, political risks, statelessness or, increasingly, the environment. Yet another reason that hinders return is belonging to a religious group outlawed or under state suspicion in the former homeland.

Some have suggested that integration can be contrasted with transnational ties and investments, something that Erdal (2013) efficiently challenges. Her conclusion is that 'state integrationism' – state programmes for integration – might feel threatened by the implications of transnationalism, but that citizenship(s) and identities need to be understood on an individual level. Her material exemplifies the research and experiences of many others, showcasing how individuals can actively participate in numerous contexts, making space in all. Her reasoning also applies to those who are engaged in transnational and global religious movements.

3.4.2 Global Religious Movements

Not all new religious movements and organisations stem from local initiatives on the part of recently arrived migrants; some are transnational or even global. The expansion of missionary movements (discussed further in Sect. 3.5.2) as a result of conscious strategies is a recurrent part of international migration. Christian Pentecostal movements, Islamic or new age Sufi movements, Jewish Chasidic movements, the Hindutva movement, Theravada Buddhism, all have made efforts to gain influence by a combination of recruiting people from co-religionists and outside (although not extensively in the Chasidic tradition).

Transnational state-driven organisations also promote their religious interpretations outside the state's territory. Saudi Arabia, for example, promotes Wahhabi Salafism by inviting European Muslims to study free of charge in Saudi Arabia, and by sending out representatives who lecture in Europe or offer – usually conditional – economic support for projects among Sunni Muslims in Europe. The Saudis also support several multi-language webpages that advertise and advise on their interpretation. Similarly, the Turkish and Moroccan states actively pursue relations with emigrant Muslims living in European states. In a country like Germany with an established Muslim population, Diyanet – the Turkish Presidency of Religious Affairs – organises by far the largest number of mosques (Nielsen & Otterbeck, 2016).

The Catholic and Protestant Churches, including the Anglican Church, must also be included in these global religious movements. Global processes and immigration now challenge Europe, the former heartland of such initiatives. Instead, previously colonised countries have formed new Christian heartlands and developed influential power centres over the last decades. As Kevin Ward states in his book on global Anglicanism, 'the way in which the black and Asian voice is esteemed, and its presence is incorporated in the life of the Church of England remains one of the most important themes for the future of Christianity in a multi-racial, secular society' (Ward, 2006: 44).

All these movements use the latest technology to broadcast their ideas. They employ media-savvy communicators and aim to influence by ideas spread through personal contact. Some of them produce popular culture, arrange sophisticated higher education or dialogues in Europe, making them interesting examples of transnational or global movements of a different sort than often is studied in social movement studies or studies of interest organisations.

3.5 Religious Services: A Crossroad of Individual and Community Tactics and Space Making

As mentioned above, the first substantial migration of followers of a particular religion requires institutionalisation in the sociological sense. Holiday rituals require or imply collective gatherings. Which space can be claimed? What can be afforded? Is there a social cost or risk to making yourself visible? These questions are important when understanding changes and processes connected to migration and religion. As seen in Chap. 2, in the US during the 1990s, there was a tendency for immigrant religious communities to adopt the US Christian form of congregations in organisational structure but also in rituals (e.g., Ebaugh, 2010; Ebaugh & Chafetz, 2000, 2002; Warner & Wittner, 1998). There are probably also changes in religious services among migrants in western European countries as these have been dominated by Christian (Protestant, Catholic and Byzantine Orthodox) churches for centuries, just as in the US case. Churches have set the scene for the institutionalisation of religion in society: which days are holidays, how and when to have religious gatherings, how religion should be taught at school, how health and criminal care are expedited and so forth. Newcomers have either adapted to this setting, changed it through political activism, *chosen* not to adapt or simply failed to initiate change in the short term. However, as the contemporary European religious scene is very complex and the establishment of immigrant religious organisations has been going on for a long time, it is difficult to claim any truly general patterns in these processes of adaptation.

If we investigate these processes from an *individual* level, we can see both an increase and decrease in religious participation among immigrants in Europe. This depends on a very wide range of factors including the countries of immigration and emigration, religion, age, gender, cohort, generation, time spent in the new home country, degree of establishment of the immigrant, the religious organisations in the new home country and reasons for emigration, among others (e.g., Van Tubergen, 2013; Van Tubergen & Sindradottir, 2011; Fleischmann & Phalet, 2012; Maliepaard et al., 2009; Crockett & Voas, 2006). In other words, there is, among immigrants, an abundance of manifest and latent reasons to change – or retain – their level of participation in religious gatherings.

The reactions from religious *communities* to such changes in participation among their (potential) adherents present the same complexity. For example, both changes and permanence in religious services depend on opportunities and work: are people willing to launch, arrange and maintain services? Further, we must keep in mind that religious participation cannot merely be understood as an 'economic' transaction depending on demand and supply (although there is admittedly some merit to this equation); there is more involved, such as theological considerations about the past, present and future of the religion, community, organisation or group. However, the starting point for these processes of change is likely to be found in changes in the immigrants' everyday realities as well as in religious services.

Religious organisations set up by immigrants have many challenges to overcome during the phase of establishment. In later phases, adaptation to keep and embrace more believers comes into greater focus, giving rise to questions such as which language to use during services (e.g., Armbruster, 2013: 68–89; Nordin, 2007) or which traditions to uphold (e.g., Sideri, 2017). In the following sections we discuss three quite different examples of religious service dynamics in response to being an immigrant or diasporic community, showing various tactics and to some extent strategies in space making.

3.5.1 Black Christian Communities in the UK and Congregational Services

In the post-war period there was an increase of immigrants from the Caribbean and West Africa to the UK, many of whom identified as Christian and black. Coming to Britain also meant joining the 'mother church' – Anglican, Methodist, Presbyterian or Baptist – to which they belonged in their countries of origin. To the disappointment of many, they felt unwelcome in these UK congregations and unable to escape feeling like intruders and strangers, something even voiced by some of the priests officiating. Racism was definitely an issue. But they also experienced congregations which they perceived to consist of members merely attending out of a sense of duty, leading to services without the enthusiasm and excitement expected by the immigrants.

Did this lead to changes in services? Yes and no. There were few changes in the established churches due to the newcomers, probably due to an unwillingness among the empowered in the congregations (members and leadership) to adapt to the new situation. Instead, successively, these immigrants created space in congregations they established themselves, many of them Pentecostal. Here they could feel more at home and at ease, find refuge, create a sense of cultural identity and be empowered. At the beginning of 1990s, over 150 Christian churches in the UK were upheld by African and Afro-Caribbean adherents. In fact, most churchgoers with this background belonged to these churches (Kalilombe, 1997).

3.5.2 Language Groups Within Migrant Communities in Sweden

The second example concerns Sweden, immigrants from Latin America and so-called language groups within Pentecostal, Catholic and Jehovah's Witnesses congregations. Instituting language groups is a common established church strategy which makes space in religious congregations in countries of settlement, offering religious services in the immigrants' mother tongue and providing opportunities for them to gather with people from the same ethnic or national background. As with the African and Afro-Caribbean churches in the UK, these groups can function as somewhere to feel at home, a refuge and a place of empowerment. The latter was shown in services pinpointing that there were theological reasons for their migration, one of which was the possibility of joining this group and evangelising in their new home country. Being part of smaller and more intimate religious services in these groups also shaped a strong sense of belonging: services were held in Spanish and in a more Latin American style; instead of the organ, guitars were played during mass in the Catholic Latin American language group. However, space making through language groups and styles was not without problems. For the second generation, religious services in Spanish were not always desirable because they did not fully understand them; thus, they tended to be divisive for the congregations, and different tactics to solve these problems were at play. However, as groups with small resources and circumscribed possibilities to influence congregations and churches, this was a challenging task (Nordin, 2007).

3.5.3 *Religious Services in Tamil Hindu Temples in Switzerland*

The third example of space making and tactics related to religious services comes from Tamil Hindu temples in Switzerland (M. Baumann, 2010). For Tamil Hindus, religious practices consist to a large extent of either individual worship at home or in temples. However, various forms of religious services offering the possibility to worship, share meals and celebrate festivals, marriages and other rites of passage are on hand in Swiss Tamil Hindu temples. Refugees, particularly from Sri Lanka, established eighteen temples in Switzerland over a period of thirty years, starting in the 1980s, which have become the main Tamil Hindu locations for religious practice in the country, largely replacing private rituals. The function of the rituals in the temples is to cultivate a sense of national and cultural belonging difficult to find elsewhere in Switzerland. Because of the sparse access to temples for the Tamil Hindus, caste separation is not practiced during worship in the temples and at meals, and the temples also offer services such as cultural events and libraries, both for Tamil Hindus and others. The tactics for space making in this case have been to offer a place for group worship and meetings, while religious services offer a place for religious, cultural and national gatherings. Changes in these services have, it seems, both been deliberate, for example having libraries, and occasional, as in meeting across castes (Baumann, 2010).

3.6 Concluding Remarks

This chapter has stressed the agency of migrants in their relations with their new societies and to religion. By first examining the micro level of individuals, and then the meso level, accentuating the establishing and administration of religious organisations, we aimed to make visible the many potential factors to be negotiated without losing sight of the people behind them. Researching migration and religion requires knowledge of the field and the ability to establish precisely what the field is, which is much more complicated today with modern communication techniques and global and transnational religious movements. It also requires the researcher to pay attention to what the migrants themselves consider important to their migration and mobility. Making space for a new religion, not least from an unprivileged position, is hard work. Establishment histories are fascinating tales of tactics, enthusiasm, conflicts and bone-headedness but also of failure, success, pride and religious commitment. Religion is important, not always, but surprisingly often, in one way or another.

References

Aktan, O. (2017). *Turkish football clubs in Berlin: An empirical study on the constitution of social positioning and ethnic belonging*. PhD thesis. Universität Potsdam. https://publishup.uni-potsdam.de/opus4-ubp/frontdoor/deliver/index/docId/41361/file/aktan_diss.pdf (Visited 20 August 2022).

Andizian, S. (1986). Women's roles in organizing symbolic life: Algerian female immigrants in France. In R. J. Simon & C. B. Brettell (Eds.), *International migration: The female experience* (pp. 254–266). New Jersey: Rowman & Allanheld.

Armbruster, H. (2013). *Keeping the faith: Syriac Christian in diaspora*. Canon Pyon: Sean Kingstone Publishing.

Baumann, M. (2010). Civic social capital and Hindu Tamil priests and temples in Switzerland. *Finnish Journal of Ethnicity and Migration, 5*(2), 33–38.

Berger, P. L., & Luckmann, T. (1966). *The social construction of reality: A treatise in the sociology of knowledge*. New York: Anchor Books.

Blaschke, J. (Ed.). (2000). *Multi-level discrimination of Muslim women in Europe*. Berlin: Edition Parabolis.

Bolognani, M., & Erdal, M. B. (2017). Return imaginaries and political climate: Comparing thinking about return mobilities among Pakistani origin migrants and descendants in Norway and the UK. *Migration & Integration, 18*, 353–367.

Breton, R. (2012). *Different gods. Integrating Non-Christian minorites*. London: McGill Queen's University Press.

Bruce, S. (2002). *God is dead: Secularization in the West*. Oxford: Blackwell.

Buruma, I. (2006). *Murder in Amsterdam: The death of Theo van Gogh and the limits of tolerance*. London: Atlantic Books.

Cato, J., & Otterbeck, J. (2014). Active citizenship among Muslims in Sweden: From minority politics to political candidacy. *Tidskrift for Islamforskning, 8*(1), 223–247.

Chen, C. (2006). From filial piety to religious piety: Evangelical Christianity reconstructing Taiwanese immigrant families in the United States. *The International Migration Review, 40*(3), 573–602.

References

Crockett, A., & Voas, D. (2006). Generations of decline: Religious change in 20th-century Britain. *Journal for the Scientific Study of Religion, 45*(4), 567–584.

Dencik, L. (1993). Hemma i hemlösheten. In J. Jakubowski (Ed.), *Judisk identitet*. Stockholm: Natur och kultur.

Dencik, L. (2009). Kosher and Christmas tree: On marriages between Jews and non-Jews in Finland, Sweden. In R. Shulamit & S. DellaPergola (Eds.), *Jewish intermarriage around the world* (pp. 75–87). London/New York: Routledge.

Dessing, N. M. (2001). *Rituals of birth, circumcision, marriage, and death among Muslims in The Netherlands*. Leuven: Peeters.

Ebaugh, H. R. (2010). Transnationality and religion in immigrant congregations: The global impact. *Nordic Journal of Religion and Society, 23*(2), 105–119.

Ebaugh, H. R., & Chafetz, J. S. (2000). *Religion and the new immigrants: Continuities and adaptations in immigrant congregations*. Walnut Creek, CA: Altamira.

Ebaugh, H. R., & Chafetz, J. S. (Eds.). (2002). *Religion across borders: Transnational immigrant networks*. Lanham: Altamira Press.

Erdal, M. B. (2013). Migrant transnationalism and multi-layered integration: Norwegian-Pakistani migrants' own reflections. *Journal of Ethnic and Migration Studies, 39*(6), 983–999.

Faist, T. (2004). The transnational turn in migration research: Perspectives for the study of politics and polity. In M. Povrzanović Frykman (Ed.), *Transnational spaces: Disciplinary perspectives*. Malmö: Malmö University.

Fesenmyer, L. (2017). Place and the (un-)making of religious peripheries: Weddings among Kenyan Pentecostals in London. In D. Garbin & A. Strhan (Eds.), *Religion and the Global City* (pp. 189–201). New York: Bloomsbury.

Fibiger, M. Q. (2017). Alike but different: The understanding of rituals among Sri Lankan Tamil Hindus in Denmark. *Journal of Ethnic and Migration Studies, 44*(16), 2634–2648.

Fleischmann, F., & Phalet, K. (2012). Integration and religiosity among the Turkish second generation in Europe: A comparative analysis across four capital cities. *Ethnic and Racial Studies, 35*(2), 320–341.

Fog Olwig, K. (2009). A proper funeral: Contextualizing community among Caribbean migrants. *Journal of the Royal Anthropological Institute, 15*(3), 520–537.

Foner, N., & Alba, R. (2008). Immigrant religion in the US and Western Europe: Bridge or barrier to inclusion? *International Migration Review, 42*(2), 360–392.

Goodhew, D., & Cooper, A.-P. (Eds.). (2019). *The desecularization of the city: London's churches, 1980 to the present*. London/New York: Routledge/Taylor and Francis.

Grønseth, A. S. (2018). Migrating rituals: Negotiations of belonging and otherness among Tamils in Norway. *Journal of Ethnic and Migration Studies, 44*(16), 2617–2633.

Hämmerli, M., & Mucha, E. (2014). Innovation in the Russian Orthodox Church: The crisis in the diocese of Sourozh in Britain. In M. Hämmerli & J.-F. Mayer (Eds.), *Orthodox identities in Western Europe: Migration, settlement and innovation* (pp. 291–302). London: Routledge.

Hirschman, C. (2004). The role of religion in the origins and adaptation of immigrant groups in the United States. *International Migration Review, 38*(3), 1206–1233.

Holm Pedersen, M. (2009). *Practices of belonging: Ritual performances and the making of place and relatedness among Iraqi women in Copenhagen*. PhD Dissertation, Department of Anthropology, University of Copenhagen.

Jacobsen, K. A., & Myrvold, K. (Eds.). (2011). *Sikhs in Europe: Migration, identities and representations*. Farnham: Ashgate.

Jakku, N. (2018). Islamophobia, representation and the Muslim political subject: A Swedish case study. *Societies, 8*(4), 1–17.

Jouili, J. S. (2015). *Pious practice and secular constraints: Women in the Islamic revival in Europe*. Stanford: Stanford University Press.

Kalilombe, P. (1997). Black Christianity in Britain. *Ethnic and Racial Studies, 20*(2), 306–324.

Kapur, D., & McHale, J. (2009). International migration and the world income distribution. *Journal of International Development, 21*(8), 1102–1110.

Karner, C., & Parker, D. (2008). Religion versus rubbish: Deprivation and social capital in inner-city Birmingham. *Social Compass, 55*(4), 517–531.

Khan, R. M. (2021). Speaking "religion" through a gender code: The discursive power and gendered-racial implications of the religious label. *Critical Research on Religion*, first online, 1–21.

Kivisto, P. (2014). *Religion and immigration: Migrant faiths in North America and Western Europe*. Malden, MA: Polity.

Knott, K. (2016). Living religious practices. In J. B. Saunders, E. Fiddian-Qamiyeh, & S. Snyder (Eds.), *Intersections of religion and migration: Religion and global migrations* (pp. 71–90). London: Palgrave Macmillan.

Levitt, P. (1998). Local-level global religion: The case of US-Dominican migration. *Journal for the Scientific Study of Religion, 37*(1), 74–89.

Levitt, P. (1999). Social remittances: A local-level, migration-driven form of cultural diffusion. *International Migration Review, 32*(4), 926–948.

Levitt, P. (2001). *The transnational villagers*. Berkeley: University of California Press.

Lorentzen, L. A., Gonzalez, J. J., III, Chun, K. M., & Do, H. D. (Eds.). (2009). *Religion at the corner of bliss and nirvana: Politics, identity, and faith in new migrant communities*. Durham: Duke University Press.

Mack, J. (2017). *The construction of equality: Syriac immigration and the Swedish city*. Minneapolis: Minnesota UP.

Magnusson, N. (2011). *Refugeeship: A project of justification: Claiming asylum in England and Sweden*. Stockholm: Stockholm University.

Maliepaard, M., Lubbers, M., & Gijsberts, M. (2009). Generational differences in ethnic and religious attachment and their interrelation: A study among Muslim minorities in The Netherlands. *Ethnic and Racial Studies, 33*(3), 451–472.

Maussen, M. (2007). Islamic presence and mosque establishment in France. *Journal of Ethnic and Migrations Studies, 33*(6), 981–1002.

Müller, J. (2014). Local relations and transnational imaginaries: Football practices of migrant men and women from Andean countries in Spain. *Soccer & Society, 15*(4), 596–617.

Nielsen, J. S., & Otterbeck, J. (2016). *Muslims in Western Europe* (4th ed.). Edinburgh: Edinburgh University Press.

Nordin, M. (2004). *Religiositet bland migranter: Sverige-chilenares förhållande till religion och samfund*. Lund: Centre for Theology and Religious Studies.

Nordin, M. (2007). Immigrant language groups in religious organisations. *Nordic Journal of Religion and Society, 1*(20), 65–86.

Nordin, M. (2017). Secularization, religious plurality, and position: Local inter-religious cooperation in contemporary Sweden. *Social Compass, 64*(3), 388–403.

Nordin, M., & Schölin, T. (2011). *Religion, vård och omsorg: Mångkulturell vård i praktiken*. Malmö: Gleerups.

Otterbeck, J. (2010a). *Samtidsislam: Unga muslimer i Malmö och Köpenhamn*. Stockholm: Carlsson.

Otterbeck, J. (2010b). Sweden: Cooperation and conflict. In A. Triandafyllidou (Ed.), *Muslims in 21st century Europe: Structural and cultural perspectives* (pp. 103–120). London: Routledge.

Otterbeck, J. (2015). "I Wouldn't call them Muslims!": Constructing a respectable Islam. *Numen, 62*(2–3), 243–264.

Petersen, J. (2020). *The making of a mosque with female imams: Serendipities, structures, and framing of Islam in Denmark*. Lund: Lund University.

Regassa, A., & Zeleke, M. (2014). Irrecha: A traditional Oromo religious ritual goes global. In A. Adogame (Ed.), *The public face of African new religious movements* (pp. 45–63). London: Routledge.

Rogers, A. (2019). Walking down the old Kent road: New Black-majority churches in the London borough of Southwark. In D. Goodhew & A.-P. Cooper (Eds.), *The desecularization of the city: London's churches, 1980 to the present*. London/New York: Routledge/Taylor and Francis.

Roy, O. (2004). *Globalized Islam: The search for a new Ummah*. New York: Columbia University Press.

References

Sa'di, A. H., & Abu-Lughod, L. (Eds.). (2007). *Nakba: Palestine, 1948, and the claims of memory*. New York: Columbia University Press.

Schielke, S. (2015). *Egypt in the future tense: Hope, frustration, and ambivalence before and after 2011*. Bloomington: Indiana University Press.

Sideri, E. (2017). Historical diasporas, religion and identity: Exploring the case of the Greeks of Tsalka. In E. Sideri & L. E. Roupakia (Eds.), *Religions and migrations in the Black Sea region* (pp. 35–56). Cham, Switzerland: Palgrave Macmillian.

Sorgenfrei, S. (2020). Establishing Islam in Sweden: The first Tatar community and Muslim congregation and their sources. *Studia Orientalia Electronica, 8*(2), 82–95.

Sparre, S. L., & Galal Paulsen, L. (2018). Incense and holy bread: The sense of belonging through ritual among Middle Eastern Christians in Denmark. *Journal of Ethnic and Migration Studies, 44*(16), 2649–2666.

Stepick, A., Rey, T., & Mahler, S. (Eds.). (2009). *Churches and charity in the immigrant city*. New Brunswick, NJ: Rutgers University Press.

Stoltz, P. (2000). *About being (T)here and making a difference: Black women and the paradox of visibility*. PhD Thesis. Lund: Lund University.

Straut-Eppsteiner, H., & Hagan, J. (2016). Religion as psychological, spiritual, and social support in the migration undertaking. In J. B. Saunders, E. Fiddian-Qasmiyeh, & S. Snyder (Eds.), *Intersections of religion and migration: Issues at the global crossroads* (pp. 49–70). New York: Palgrave/Springer.

Van Tubergen, F. (2013). Religious change of new immigrants in The Netherlands: The event of migration. *Social Science Research, 42*(3), 715–725.

Van Tubergen, F., & Sindradóttir, J. (2011). The religiosity of immigrants in Europe: A cross-National Study. *Journal for the Scientific Study of Religion, 50*(2), 272–288.

Waardenburg, J. (1978). Official and popular religion in Islam. *Social Compass, 25*(3–4), 315–341.

Waardenburg, J. (1983). The right to ritual: Mosques in The Netherlands. *Nederlands Theologisch Tijdschrift, 37*(3), 253–264.

Ward, K. (2006). *A history of global Anglicanism*. Cambridge: Cambridge University Press.

Warner, S., & Wittner, J. (Eds.). (1998). *Gatherings in diaspora: Religious communities and the new immigration*. Philadelphia: Temple University Press.

Werbner, P. (2003). *Pilgrims of love: The anthropology of a global Sufi cult*. London: Hurst & Company.

Yang, F. (1998). Chinese conversion to evangelical Christianity: The importance of social and cultural contexts. *Sociology of Religion, 59*(3), 237–257.

Open Access This chapter is licensed under the terms of the Creative Commons Attribution 4.0 International License (http://creativecommons.org/licenses/by/4.0/), which permits use, sharing, adaptation, distribution and reproduction in any medium or format, as long as you give appropriate credit to the original author(s) and the source, provide a link to the Creative Commons license and indicate if changes were made.

The images or other third party material in this chapter are included in the chapter's Creative Commons license, unless indicated otherwise in a credit line to the material. If material is not included in the chapter's Creative Commons license and your intended use is not permitted by statutory regulation or exceeds the permitted use, you will need to obtain permission directly from the copyright holder.

Chapter 4
Negotiating Space: Strategies of the European States and Politics of Religion

In this chapter addresses how space making in relation to migrants' religions is negotiated from the perspective of the receiving countries. In this chapter, we stress the difference between tactics, as social power practices among the less influential, and the strategies practiced by more influential social agents when establishing space, that is, the social practice of place. Thus, the space making tactics in focus in Chap. 3 here make way for discussion of strategies of space making by social agents who are likely to be able to assert and practice power in influential ways. In this case, these are states, regional and local authorities in the country of residence and more abstract social institutions such as political, juridical and educational systems.

To complement this perspective, we present useful theories from political science that make some crucial structures visible. In an influential book, political scientists Joel Fetzer and Christopher Soper (2005) set out to test how France, Germany and the UK have succeeded (or not) in accommodating the religious needs of Muslims, presenting four possible approaches: resource mobilisation theory, political opportunity structure theory, political ideological theories and the importance of church-state history.

The first theory focuses on the effects of successful or poor mobilisation by an interest group, in this case Muslims and their organisations, in competition with others. What alliances are made? What political capital can be created out of the mobilisation of resources (money, labour, people)? There is an affinity with social movement theories.

The second theory centres on how available legal, institutional, social and political structures may create or block opportunities for the political mobilisation of an interest group. It also suggests that achieving group goals is dependent on the political structures produced by institutions.

The third theory looks closely at how the political ideology of states – and especially ideas about citizenship, integration and plurality – might impact on an interest group's opportunities. This again changes the focus, in this case from the group and state institutions to the importance of political ideology.

Finally – with the help of the findings of their study – Fetzer and Soper modify the theories by pointing out that 'inherited' socio-political church-state structures should be considered, as these form essential conditions for institutional structures, political ideologies and patterns of mobilisation.

Bellow we address this as the politics of religion. While modified versions of theory two and three have a strong explanatory value, Fetzer and Soper find that resource mobilisation theory cannot solely explain the accommodation of Muslims in the studied countries.

There are some weaknesses in their otherwise solid argumentation. The approach is a political science one, looking at structures over a fairly short period, and fails to illuminate the long-term hard work of religious individuals and organisations (i.e., resource mobilisation) that has, at times, led to changes in structures and ideologies. An illustrative example is the lobbying by Muslims and Jews in different states for a change in laws regulating slaughter and the accessibility to halal and kosher food in institutions such as schools, hospitals and prisons. By participating on committees, writing responses in the public sphere and making demands, and by doing so continuously over time, the situation for those who want halal or kosher slaughtered meat but accept non-fatal pre-stunning of the animals to be slaughtered has improved vastly over a period of 50 years. However, it has proved a pricey victory as it has provided antisemitic and Islamophobic activists with a tool with which to attack Jews and Muslims (e.g., Linehan, 2012; Nielsen & Otterbeck, 2016).

Yet another issue lacking attention in Fetzer's and Soper's study are relations between the state and domestic ethnic and religious minorities which run parallel with church-state history. For example, without such analysis, we may fail to understand the full background and importance of the proclamation by the Swedish state in 1975 that in future it would accept and promote multiculturalism. Among the most powerful lobbyists for this change was the Sámi population (the indigenous population in the north), not the new immigrants, whose numbers were still low at the time. The success of the Sámi, in turn, was highly dependent on the severe discrimination they experienced from the Swedish state and the increased political awareness of this injustice, yet migrants could also benefit from new political opportunity structures created by a change in ideology closely related to the resource mobilisation of the indigenous group (e.g., Cato, 2012; Lundgren, 2021).

Below, keeping Fetzer and Soper's framework as reference, we first discuss the importance of the politics of religion over time, culminating in a contemporary example. We then discuss various legal issues related to religion, as these illustrate how the politics of religion can be implemented. The chapter ends with an overview of complex areas where the politics of religion leads to conflicts but may also render social cohesion: public institutions, antisemitism and islamophobia, securitisation and interfaith groups.

Our goal with the chapter is to *complement* Chap. 3 individual and group perspective with a state perspective, to present a richer understanding of religion and migration in Europe. Both research and public debates sometimes risk a primary focus on the questions and needs of states, excluding the needs, let alone the perspectives, of immigrants.

4.1 Politics of Religion in History and Today

In this part we accentuate the importance of focusing on the politics of religion, both in the present and, to a degree, the past, when studying post-1950 religion and migration. All European states have political strategies on religion, suggesting the prominent position of religions, although sometimes France is claimed to be an exception. This is folly. On the contrary, France is an interesting and illustrative case, with a very active politics of religion, mostly aimed at thwarting the influence of religious stakeholders. The relationship between the French state and the Catholic Church is regulated by a law dating from 9 December 1905, which, among other things, guarantees 'freedom of conscience' and the 'free exercise of religion'. Of course, this applies to migrants too. Further, the state is responsible for the maintenance of churches that existed before 1905. However, in Alsace-Lorraine, a territory of France that has been alternately under French and German rule, old laws apply (the Concordat of 1801). In that region, the French state acknowledges certain named religions, a rather unusual arrangement in western Europe, but common in central and eastern Europe. The Concordat recognises three branches of Christianity (Catholicism, Lutheranism and Calvinism) and Judaism. Unlike the rest of France, the state pays the salaries of the clergy of these religions, organises religious education at state schools and provides for two theological faculties, one Catholic and one Protestant, at Strasbourg University. Attempts have been made to expand the category of recognised religions to include others, but to date these have failed. Nevertheless, Strasbourg University has been proactive and since 2014 has arranged training for Muslim imams centred on law, history and sociology. Further, even though the French state celebrates its own take on secularism, *laïcité*, and excludes religion from the state school curriculum altogether (except in Alsace-Lorraine, as mentioned), the Catholic Church is allowed, as the only religious denomination, to arrange private schools that affirm religion (e.g., Fetzer & Soper, 2005; Nielsen & Otterbeck, 2016).

It should be clear from this brief example that the politics of religion matters and that one needs to consider not only the claimed ideology of a state but also the actual practices in all their possibly contradictory forms. Moreover, studying the history of European states reveals the importance of religion(s) in the legitimation of power in laws, in the understanding of governance of religion in different public institutions such as education and healthcare, in religious conflicts and as part of the political and religious values of politicians.

4.1.1 The Westphalian Settlement

European religious politics are deeply rooted in history. As the prominence of multiculturalism in European politics grew from the mid-1970s until the early twenty-first century – in attempts to develop a durable political response to religious, cultural and ethnic diversity – it met firm resistance from conservatives and, later, from principally right-wing populists. Scholars claim the opposition originates in the political cognitive maps that have affected many Europeans' political perceptions since the Westphalian Settlement of 1648 (e.g., Nexon, 2006). The trauma of the Thirty Years' War led to attempts to formulate principals that would hinder future atrocities, efforts which, in terms of religion, found expression in the famous Latin phrase, *cuius regio, eius religio*, meaning that the religion of the ruler of a territory decides the religious belonging of those ruled. A principal borrowed from the 1555 Peace of Augsburg, it firmly established the idea of national churches, efficiently destroying future dreams of a politically united European Catholic Christendom.

The development and consolidation of national churches, assumed to dominate the same territory as a state, and the ensuing assumption that a proper citizen belonged to the national church, fashioned an implicit (sometimes explicit) normality. It also created severe problems for migrants of other faiths or Christian denominations who had to face social, legal, political and theological discrimination perceived as justified by the vast majority of any given state's population and administration. It goes without saying that domestic national religious minorities also often suffered from this nationalistic politics of religion, although every state has its own trajectory in relation to this common history. When European nations became colonial powers, the national church model and the idea of the nation state were parts of the taken-for-granted status quo that followed colonialisation, thus affecting the politics of religion among colonialised people (e.g., Beyer, 2022).

When studying the politics of religion and migration to Europe, the legal, political and social aspects of citizenship must be considered; theoretical observations that are not anchored in history seldom reach relevant conclusions. Thus, any research project needs a grounded diachronic and synchronic knowledge of the field studied.

4.1.2 The Neighbourhood, the State, or the Transnational?

A word of caution is in order. Andreas Wimmer and Nina Glick Schiller (2002) have minted the term 'methodological nationalism', to alert the researcher to be cautious about whether the field they are studying is really the state. Researchers need to reflect on rescaling (Glick Schiller & Çağlar, 2009) to find the relevant scale of their field. At times, a study might be about a region of a state, a neighbourhood in a city, a federal union or, indeed, transnational connections between religious groups and their members in several, cities, regions or states. An example of this is Petr Kratochvíl and Tomáš Doležal's (2015) study of the Catholic Church in Europe and its relations with the European Union, which explores processes of secularisation in contemporary societies, underlining the importance of the difference between institutions and organisations. In a similar vein, John Bowen et al. (2014) stress that an institution (in the sociological sense) might have a 'relative autonomy' to the state or other institutions, something to be taken into account by scholars studying it. Institutions like the military, schools or healthcare should not be assumed to have the same relations with a national model or ideology (for example, French *laïcité*). Further, as with all important issues, there will be a variety of preferred political solutions in every country. Thus, a wide knowledge of overlapping contexts and cognitive maps is important when selecting the right scale of the field.

4.1.3 Governances of Religion(s)

The politics of religion and migration is often manifested in the governance of religions. Let us first explain the background of this. One of the main concerns of a state is to manage its population and, as it changes due to migration, new challenges are likely to appear. When it comes to religion, these can be met in many ways. States may or may not try to include migrants by acknowledging their religious institutions or practices, while, presumably, there are practices that the state would like migrants to adopt and those that the state encourages, accepts or consciously does not want to impede. Roger Waldinger (2007: 347) addresses this as 'political resocialisation', which cleverly moves the conceptualisation away from the integration debate. To enable it to take control of processes of resocialisation, the state will use statistics, legal measures, education, surveillance (see Sect. 4.3.2.2) and policies – often packaged in the frame of projects (e.g., Messner, 2015).

Tuomas Martikainen (2014) has introduced the concept of 'the project society' in migration studies – borrowing it from political science – to characterise the administrative type typical of the neo-liberal state. The idea is that organisations (or individual citizens) are encouraged to apply for grants to conduct projects in line with the views of the grant giver instead of receiving continuous support, meaning that religious organisations, including immigrant ones, must adjust to the political opportunity structure of the project society. The economic benefits of landing a project are important for the survival of organisations, as most have a restricted economy, making them partners in projects connected with local democracy, equality and integration. States strategise to take control over processes of resocialisation among immigrants and govern religious organisations, and projects may be covert or overt attempts to achieve this, meanwhile shifting the responsibility for implementation from state authorities to religious organisations.

The state governance of the religious organisations of immigrants, through projects or in other ways, is often challenged by the lack of detailed knowledge about the religious belongings of immigrants. In fact, most European states have legislation that forbids or hinders the registration of its citizens' religious preferences. Instead, such information is gathered on the basis of self-identification, first added to the UK census in 2001, while Switzerland has conducted a census containing a religion question every ten years since 1850 and Sweden has had its membership statistics since 1975. In the latter case, the statistics do not cover large groups of religiously non-organised migrants. No European state prints the religious identity of its citizens on ID cards any longer, although in the past both Greece (1945–2001) and (Euro-Asian) Turkey (prior to 2016) have done so.

There is, however, another tradition, mainly involving the states of former Eastern Europe, where religion is registered and connected with specific rights. For example, the Romanian state registers its citizens' religious affiliation if they are prepared to provide it, which all but 6.25 percent (census 2011) have been prepared to do. The Romanian state recognises a number of religions (including Judaism and Islam) and adherents of those faiths have some specified rights according to law (see Sect. 4.2.1), which are not extended to non-citizens.

Clearly, a lack of statistics creates problems for the governance of religions; without this information, it is harder for everyday bureaucracy to plan the budgets and logistics of seemingly simple things like free school lunches: how many kids can be expected to ask for a kosher or halal diet at school? Similarly, not knowing how many adherents there are of different denominations makes it difficult for the authorities to evaluate the relevance of demands for special treatment – regarding prayer facilities, diets, holidays or dress at work, in the army, at school or in prisons – raised by religious activists, parents, pupils, employees, inmates and others. It is especially difficult when demographics change.

We must also be aware (see Sect. 4.1.2), that governance of religion no longer takes place only on a national level or only between state authorities and religious organisations. With reference to Anne Mette Kjær's *Governance* (2004), Mel Prideaux and Andrew Dawson (2018) argue that contemporary Western governance of religion is highly dynamic and includes additional institutions, such as non-governmental agencies, private enterprises, majority churches and charitable institutions, and involves various forms of collaboration, consultation and innovation; sensitivity is required to navigate this very complex field.

4.2 Rights, Obligations and Laws

Legalisation offers a concrete example of the implementation of politics of religion. One may easily get the impression that the laws of European states are simply centred on the rights and obligations of the individual citizen, but the politics of religion often implies collective rights, occasionally particularism, when specific rights are allocated to different groups. It tends to translate into laws that come in three major forms: those acknowledging certain religious groups and assigning them status and rights; those that guarantee the freedom of religion of citizens who choose to act collectively; and those, like blasphemy and anti-discrimination laws, that aim to protect religion or religious groups from being subjected to hatred, scorn and sometimes ridicule.

4.2.1 Acknowledging Religious Group Rights

Romania and Germany provide two interesting, very different cases of group rights. Romania acknowledges eighteen 'cults' including sixteen Christian denominations (Jehovah's Witnesses since 2008), Jewish communities and Islam, giving them all specific rights laid down in law. A recognised religious cult may receive government grants, calculated on the basis of the number of members, to cover costs related to staff salaries and the maintenance or construction of sanctuaries. Once recognised, it also has the right to establish schools, teach its religion in state schools, promote its faith on radio and TV and broadcast as community radio. Further, religious cults are exempt from taxation. Romania also recognises national religious organisations instituted by the 'cults', and their heads, making it one of the few non-Muslim European countries that has a state-employed head of the Muslim community (*Muftiatul Cultului Musulman din România*). These rights are as extensive as any in Europe, not counting those of state churches, although it has been reported that they are not upheld without friction, and that discrimination against individuals is widespread (e.g., Iordache, 2004).

Germany's constitution is termed *religionsneutral*. Still, German law gives specific rights to *Körperschaft des öffentlichen Rechts*, that is, recognised religious corporations, a status long held by Protestant churches, the Catholic dioceses and the Jewish community. It comes with many rights, with the state administering the collection of 'church taxes' or membership fees and allowing the corporations to run nursery schools, hospitals and welfare institutions. In fact, to a large extent the state depends on this; for example, churches run 50 percent of all publicly funded nursery schools. Other religious communities, organising as associations or foundations, do not have the same rights as the recognised corporations.

To make up a recognised religious corporation in the eyes of the law, it must have existed for at least 30 years and most members should be German citizens. Up until 2000, German citizenship laws were built on the principle of *ius sanguinis* (the right of blood), not *ius soli* (the rights of soil), that is, citizenship was dependent on people being considered part of the 'German people', not on their living in Germany or not. In 2000, Germany began to allow naturalisation under rather ungenerous rules that included the renunciation of former citizenships. Nonetheless, many of the older migrants, considered 'guest workers' up until then, met the requirements, which transformed the sizeable Muslim population in Germany from mainly foreigners residing in Germany into Muslim German citizens. Due to this, the first two decades of the twenty-first century have seen tremendous changes. Muslims have been given the rights to teach their religion to Muslim children at schools in most *Bundesländer* – Germany is a federation allowing for different rules regionally. To meet the demand for new teachers, six German universities have started higher education training in Islamic theology. Thus, a change in the political ideology of citizenship provided the political opportunity structures for migrants with a long presence in Germany to gain certain religious collective rights (e.g., Nielsen & Otterbeck, 2016).

4.2.2 Freedom of Religion

The second typical trait is freedom of religion legislation, a highly complex legal area flaunting a symbolic proclamation at its centre but entrapped and entangled in a myriad detailed restrictions and rulings, rendering citizens less free than implied by the proclamation. Freedom of religion consists of two aspects: an individual right – freedom to and from religion – and a collective right – the freedom to gather, hold services and be acknowledged as organisations, at times with specific rights as mentioned above. In European states, the religious collective has the right to make (some) collective decisions free of outside domination, but has no legal means to force an individual whom the group may consider 'belongs' to the community to participate or belong.

The nuances of freedom of religion differ from one state to another although it is conditional in all European legislation, both national and on an EU level, in that people are not allowed to disturb the peace; moreover, it is subordinate to other laws regarding, for example, the economy, marriage and slaughter. In some cases, religious organisations are given *carte blanche* to discriminate in workplaces in ways not tolerated from other employers, exemplified by the right to exclude women from certain religious professions. At other times, specific states have laws restricting quotidian religious rites in public that ritualise the body, as discussed above.

Freedom of religion legislation is one of those church-state history infused political ideologies that also create political opportunity structures. Apart from enjoying the freedom to organise crucial for many religious migrants, not least those from discriminated-against minorities, political activity among migrants in this field is often about blasphemy and anti-discrimination.

4.2.3 Blasphemy and Anti-discrimination Laws

Laws to protect religions or religious people comprise the third typical trait of the politics of religion. In Europe (if counting Russia and Turkey) in 2021, thirteen countries have blasphemy laws, or the equivalent thereof, while if we go back to 2000, we find twenty-one countries with such legislation. Finland, for example, has a blasphemy law, dating from 1922, which defines a blasphemer as someone who 'publicly blasphemes against God or, for the purpose of offending, publicly defames or desecrates what is otherwise held to be sacred by a church or religious community, as referred to in the Act on the Freedom of Religion (267/1922)'; breaking this law may lead to fines. While rarely used, it was last tested in 2009 in a court case in which the right-wing politician, Jussi Kristian Halla-Aho, was fined 330€ for 'disturbing worship' with a blog post linking Muhammed and Islam to paedophilia. The post also slighted Muslim Somali immigrants by connecting them to criminality. Halla-Aho stated the post was ironically modelled on a post making absurd claims about Finns and violence. Later, the ruling was confirmed by the Supreme Court, which increased the fine to 400€.

In Europe in general, it is highly uncommon for any religious group consisting mainly of recent migrants to win a court case involving blasphemy, often because the laws in question are dormant and few politicians or judges want to re-activate them – with the exception of Georgia which is discussing the introduction of a blasphemy law. Another reason is that laws may only protect specific religions and exclude those of migrants, such as the blasphemy law in England and Wales, abolished in 2008, protecting only the Church of England. Thirdly, migrant communities tend initially not to have enough contacts, know-how, influence and finance to enforce the law, even if they have a case. This is changing as migrant communities become settled and established, and there have been a number of– largely unsuccessful – cases in Europe where Muslims have tried to enforce the blasphemy laws.

Thus, the situation in Europe is that blasphemy laws are dormant or repealed, although it may be more correct to argue that they have been replaced with discrimination laws, especially within the EU. While blasphemy laws were disappearing during the first two decades of the 2000s, discrimination laws were being amended, with clauses touching on religious discrimination. This is exemplified by Swedish discrimination legislation where, in the late 1990s, religious belonging was mainly mentioned as a subcategory of ethnicity; due to criticism from the EU, however, in 2008 religion was pronounced one of seven possible grounds for discrimination.

4.3 Getting to Know Each Other and Areas of Conflicts

Comparing the US and European countries, scholars have continuously come to the same conclusions: being religiously active has a bridging function in the US, while it is more of a barrier in Europe (e.g., Foner & Alba, 2008; Kivisto, 2014). Kivisto points out other factors, not least that the established population in a country views newcomers through preconceived notions about ethnic groups, 'race' and religions. On a general level, populations of the various European countries differ considerably in how they value newcomers, and it changes over time. For example, Polish migrants have experienced a stark change for the worse in England and Ireland over the last two decades; Finnish migrants to Sweden have long been exposed to the stereotype of Finns as particularly prone to hard liquor drinking and violence, while the ethnic group that constantly ends up as the least tolerated in attitude surveys across Europe is the Roma people. But at least most Polish, Finish and Roma migrants are Christian and come from within Europe, while migrants from outside Europe espouse religions about which established residents may know little or nothing beyond an unfavourable impression.

Many scholars have made it clear that country-wide, regional and local authorities – founded and generally dominated by the established population – tend to reproduce preconceived ethnic and religious notions about newcomers, especially initially. Below, we address some central themes in the processes whereby authorities and migrants of different religions become acquainted.

4.3.1 Religion in Public Institutions

Post-WWII immigration has meant that European states have had to handle a more plural religious situation; the former majority church setting can no longer be taken for granted. The religious changes caused by immigration surprised European politicians and others in the receiving countries, who, in one way or another, had internalised the idea of secular states, or even non-religious lives, due to ongoing secularisation processes. For many immigrants, the idea of secular states, including religious freedom laws, have been pull factors for emigration but this does not have to coincide with a wish to live a non-religious life, either privately or in the public sphere. Therefore, politicians were confronted with the question of how to include or restrict immigrants' religious practices in countries where religion was understood to be vanishing or, at least, only taking place in private spheres. Simultaneously, the majority religion was present in everyday normality, yet somewhat invisible, as is common of the taken-for-granted. The situation has become very complex and instigates constant negotiations of space (e.g., Mattes et al., 2016).

In the following two sections we discuss examples of this private-public crossroads in which negotiations of space have been lively in Europe in recent decades, and present various strategies in the politics of religion used by the state authorities. One focuses on educational systems, the other on health care.

4.3.1.1 Educational Systems

European countries have had different strategies for teaching in and about Islam in relation to Muslim pupils over time that revolve around the questions of whether schools should affirm religious identity and how to foster tolerant (non-Islamophobic) citizens. These strategies differ 'from country to country and region to region due to diversity of political systems, histories and cultures, variety in relationships between religion and state, differing educational cultures, and also the heterogeneous nature of Muslim populations' (Ipgrave et al., 2010: 75).

In the UK, strategies for handling teaching in and about Islam at schools have a long history (e.g., Anwar, 1988). Due to residence patterns among Muslims in the UK (the largest proportion with Pakistani, Bangladeshi and Indian ancestry), inner-city community schools tend to have many Muslim pupils, sometimes a majority. There are also independent Muslim schools and a small proportion of state-maintained Muslim schools, all with a Muslim majority. Julia Ipgrave et al. (2010) demonstrate the different strategies in managing the needs and wishes of these Muslim pupils and their parents, comparing three primary schools, all with a Muslim majority. In the first, an independent Muslim school, teaching is in Islam, which is the starting point and guides the needs of the pupils (all being Muslims). In one of the inner-city schools, the point of departure is secular; religion has little place in school life and is in general seen as something primarily private. In the religious education classes, Islam is not treated any differently from other religions and emphasis is placed on commonalities among them. In the third school – also an inner-city community school but with a higher proportion of Muslim pupils than the former – the strategy towards Islam is complex and not always clear. There are ongoing processes in which the Muslim pupils' religion is taken into consideration; however, this is done with the help of external Muslim advisers and mediators, changing the power structures in this school. Thus, in a seemingly homogeneous public arena, various strategies for space making can be found (see also Jaffe-Walter, 2013; Rissanen, 2012).

The rooms of silence (or multi-faith prayer rooms) at universities are an interesting arena for space making in educational settings, one scrutinised by Hoeg et al. (2019) at Scandinavian universities in relation to secularisation processes and increasing religious plurality. The study illustrates the different strategies implemented by the universities. The Scandinavian countries have a largely common religious structure (i.e., homogenous; Protestant majority churches have faced scattered religious plurality due to substantial migration only in recent decades), are politically similar (a long history of democracy and monarchies) and have a higher-education sector dominated by state-run universities. Yet reasons for the establishment of rooms of silence at universities and changes in them (including where to place them, who can use them and their furnishing) vary between the three countries. What is most striking is that management of the rooms of silence includes both written policies and agreements and, in many ways more 'hidden', tactics by the users, evident in the ways the rooms are decorated and used, with the latter influencing space making as much as formal strategies.

4.3.1.2 Health Care Systems

The second sphere where the private-public religion dichotomy is clearly at play is the health care sector: those responsible for health care, those who receive health care and those working at health care institutions. The receiving states' strategies in handling a more religious pluralistic situation in this sector are like those related to the educational system, dependent on country, region, political system, histories and cultures, religion-state relations, differing health care cultures and heterogeneity in religions. If we inspect, for example, the arrangement of rooms of silence (in the health care system often knows as chapels, or worship, prayer or quiet rooms), we find similar processes as mentioned above (e.g., Gilliat-Ray, 2005; Nordin, 2018).

In their study of hospitals in Spain, Julia Martínez-Ariño and Mar Griera (2016) demonstrate how hospital strategies related to religious plurality are caught between formal regulations, processes of democratisation and secularisation, a scientific biomedical model, historical religious traditions and the patient autonomy model. In Spain, the law states that public hospitals shall secure religious freedom and provide onsite possibilities for religious practices; however, there are no national regulations or policies guiding how this should be done. This has led to pragmatic case-by-case solutions in which the Catholic Church, due to its majority, historical position and recourse access, can more easily, but not without resistance from the health care promotors, provide religious care at hospitals. The situation for religious minorities, with less time in the country and fewer resources, is more difficult and still developing, although one common route to their inclusion is with the help of hospital employees and, in some cases, the Catholic Church. Martínez-Ariño and Griera conclude that in hospitals in Spain 'there is no straightforward institutional response to religious diversity, but rather complex and non-linear processes of adjustment' (p. 39).

4.3.2 Conflict Areas and (Desired) Social Cohesion

States are aware of possible and actual tensions between the established population and the migrants of new religions, or between migrants of different religions; a part of governance is to try to manage such situations. Below we pursue three themes in which these tensions become clear: antisemitism and Islamophobia; securitisation and radicalisation; and interfaith initiatives. It is common for states to act in concert with civil society organisations to reduce tension or to mitigate what are seen as risks.

4.3.2.1 Antisemitism and Islamophobia

Most European states, if not all their political parties, pursue social cohesion as a goal. They attempt to educate their populations on antisemitism and Islamophobia through exhibitions, printed material, sponsored research and the curricula at schools and universities. At times, states reach out to Jewish and Muslim groups, involving them in projects, dialogues (see Sect. 4.3.2.3) or police protection programmes.

However, the antisemitism and Islamophobia of European states run deep and are part of the history of mainline churches, politics, colonialism, racism, university research and educations. It is impossible in the space here to engage with the history; instead, we discuss the political discourse, legal frameworks and attempts to control antisemitism and Islamophobia in society. Evidently, other prejudices can affect religious migrants. This includes Christophobia, mainly targeting non-established or minority forms of Christianity, and different forms of positive or negative exoticizing discourses on Hinduism or Buddhism.

It is common to see antisemitism and Islamophobia as racism, and, indeed, historian George Fredrickson (2002: 33) traces the background of racism to Christian conquest of the Iberian Peninsula in the fifteenth century and the ensuing Spanish discourse on the 'purity of blood' which could be tainted by neither Jews nor Muslims. Still, while assumed 'races' have no real content, religions have. Admittedly, religious discourse is contradictory in its vast plurality, but there *is* content, and antisemitism and Islamophobia often target alleged content. This dimension should be researched. Obviously, some forms of antisemitism and Islamophobia comprise discrimination along the same lines as general racism.

The Holocaust and the moral positioning of working against antisemitism provide a moral compass regarding the limits of tolerance in a great deal of state-driven political discourse (e.g., Romeyn, 2014). Yet antisemitism is prevalent in the far right and frequent accusations of antisemitism are directed towards the left, which tends to deny such allegations. However, when it comes to Islamophobia, political conversations across Europe feature rather mainstream parties that readily admit to seeing Muslims as uniquely problematic people and Islam as a dangerous political ideology. A study of Swedish political discourse (Cato, 2012) demonstrates that there was a turn in 1989 (caused by the Rushdie Affair) when the first speech in the Swedish parliament mentioning Muslims as belonging to a different (less valued) civilisation was made; previously, Muslims had only been mentioned in contexts where religious identity was relevant, such as when discussing religion in education. Since then, discourse has oscillated between understanding and tolerance, and rejection and fearmongering, culminating in the political discourse of the Sweden Democrats – part of the new populist, nationalist trend in European politics – and their breakthrough in 2010 as one of the larger parties.

Differences in the attitudes of European states to antisemitism and Islamophobia can, as already noted, be observed in legal frameworks. While antisemitism may be specifically regulated by law (e.g., by criminalising any denial of the Holocaust, the course followed by sixteen European countries), Islamophobia is generally regulated by discrimination laws. Commonly, both are 'hate crimes' that may be considered to aggravate circumstances. In all European countries it is within the rights of the citizen to criticise religions, but less acceptable to criticise their adherents collectively (see Sect. 4.2.3).

4.3.2.2 Securitisation as a Response to (Perceived) Radicalisation

Radicalisation is a word increasingly used from the early twenty-first century and is defined by the UK Home Office (2011) as, 'The process by which people come to support terrorism and violent extremism and, in some cases, then join terrorist groups.' Securitisation is the political discourse on how to govern radicalised people, mainly by monitoring alleged extremists and preventing extremism from growing through surveillance. At best, such securitisation hinders acts of terror and, at worst, creates fear and hatred of the surveying authorities among those deemed potential risks. However, programmes like the UK's PREVENT tend to do both and much more.

PREVENT was introduced in 2003 as part of CONTEST, a British counter-terrorism strategy, and was made public in 2006. It is one of several similar programmes developed in the EU, albeit one of the most far-reaching. Intentionally or not, the UK government has created a feeling of being monitored among Muslim migrants and UK Muslims at large. The failure to separate between conservative Islam and political interests informed by Islam or religious belonging on the one hand, and radicalisation leading to security threats on the other, were acknowledged in an evaluation ordered by the government and published in 2011 (PREVENT Strategy, 2011). Securitisation has given rise to vulnerability narratives among UK Muslims, that is, narratives about being exposed, monitored, made suspicious and unfairly treated simply for being Muslim. PREVENT is an ongoing programme fighting an uphill battle to get Muslim organisations to collaborate, mostly due to its insensitive launching (e.g., Cole, 2009; Enayat, 2020).

Still, it is very likely that fresh acts of terror will be committed on European soil by people who self-identify as Muslims and are motivated by global ideologies connected to Islamic political groups, accompanied by the presence of troops from European countries in conflicts where such groups are involved. And, as any government would want to prevent violent acts as far as possible, Muslim migrants are particularly targeted as possible security threats and questioned and put under surveillance. This situation has been critically assessed by a number of researchers (e.g., Rosenow-Williams, 2014; Goli & Rezaei, 2011), who have presented a balanced criticism of state securitisation.

It must also be pointed out that many Muslim communities work hard against radicalisation, at times in cooperation with government initiatives and the police. Mosque activists frequently describe confronting radical preachers and other militants trying to propagate in mosques or even take them over. It must equally be acknowledged that some Muslim organisations have been naïve in their dualist preaching of good and evil, polarising themselves and the West or the majority society in which they live, while failing to see the possible effects on adherents. Finally, some have actually recruited and trained adherents to turn to political violence (e.g., Inge, 2017; Nesser, 2015). Researchers will have to be sensitive to the possibility of overlapping motives, discrimination, politically disciplinary mechanisms, racism and so much more in this sensitive field. They will also have to reflect ethically on their own role and social position in relation to the state and the surveyed.

Part of the governance of religion involves trying to steer adherence away from unwanted religious expressions through interfaith dialogue initiated both by states and religious groups, to which we now turn.

4.3.2.3 Interfaith Groups

It is important to consider the interfaith sector when attempting to understand areas of potential conflict and the complex relations between state strategies and individual or group tactics in the politics of religion. This is particularly significant when it comes to the public governance of interfaith groups. In western Europe, there has been a significant growth of various interfaith initiatives during recent decades, the premises of which are mostly shaped by immigration and the ensuing religious plurality. Religious organisations are not solely responsible for initiating and upholding such programmes; rather, it is the public sector –municipalities and governments – which has to a large degree encouraged interfaith groups to govern religious plurality by fostering inclusion and social cohesion. However, we should keep in mind the various strategies on different levels involved in these processes and also that the outcome is not always inclusive (e.g., Nordin, 2020, 2017; Galal Paulsen et al., 2018; Griera & Nagel, 2018; Klinkhammer et al., 2011).

This complexity can be seen in a qualitative study based on research of the governance of state-interfaith groups in two parts of Germany: Hamburg and the Rhine-Ruhr metropolitan area (Körs & Nagel, 2018),[1] which have a high degree of religious plurality due to immigration. However, Körs and Nagel demonstrate both difference and similarities in strategies, and partly tactics, in the negotiation of religious space when it comes to interfaith groups. While governance of interfaith is a growing phenomenon in the two regions, it varies and is closely connected to context. Yet a common feature was the importance of the established churches in the governance of the groups. Having the resources, and in a way being extensions of the state or having 'quasi-state agency' (p. 357), the established churches had the ability to initiate and support these groups, which gave them influence but also enabled the other religions represented in the groups to gain leverage in relation to the state; 'the structural asymmetry turned into a strategic partnership' (p. 357). A final common pattern was the selection of religions to include in these state-interfaith groups: the focus was often on 'world religions'. This meant that some religions had no chance of being included and also that religions with (very) few members (e.g., Buddhism, Hinduism, Judaism) had the same number of representatives in the groups as religious groups with many members (e.g., Islam). A further problem is that both Islam and Christianity contain numerous different groups, some that cooperate easily and some that would not be caught dead in the same room, a characteristic that is, to a certain extent, true of all religions (apart from a few new ones). It is always interesting when research uncovers who is included, who is excluded and why.

4.4 Concluding Remarks

The four theories that feature in Fetzer and Soper's work represent the processes engaged in by immigrant religious groups and the host states. Unlike Fetzer and Soper, we would like to note the important work of many religious immigrant activists in the formation of state politics; however, it would be naïve to stipulate an *a priori* influence because of their engagement. On the contrary, an important part of research is to demonstrate the facts on the ground by thorough empirical study. That involves considering this kind of activism as it has the potential to change and challenge invisible normalities, although it is often the crushing power of states that decides the way forward.

---

[1] In Germany, much of the state governance of interfaith initiatives is implemented by the 16 Bundesländer, and is consequently very varied.

References

Anwar, M. (1988). Muslim community and the issues in education. In B. O'Keeffe (Ed.), *Schools for tomorrow: Building walls or building bridges* (pp. 80–100). London: Falmer Press.

Beyer, P. (2022). Global migration, religious diversity and integration in regions of the West: Challenging a "Westphalian" circumstance. In R. Ramji & A. Marshall (Eds.), *The Bloomsbury handbook of religion and migration* (pp. 9–24). London: Bloomsbury.

Bowen, J., Bertossi, C., Duyvendak, J. W., & Krook, M. L. (Eds.). (2014). *European states and their Muslim citizens: The impact of institutions on perceptions and boundaries*. Cambridge: Cambridge University Press.

Cato, J. (2012). *När islam blev svenskt: Föreställningar om islam och muslimer i svensk offentlig politik 1975–2010*. PhD Thesis. Lund University.

Cole, D. (2009). English lessons: A comparative analysis of UK and US responses to terrorism. *Current Legal Problems, 62*(1), 136–167.

Enayat, H. (2020). UK think-tanks, the war on terror and the radicalisation debate. In *Abdou Filali-Ansary occasional paper series* (Vol. No. 4). Aga Khan University – Institute for the Study of Muslim Civilisations.

Fetzer, J. S., & Soper, J. C. (2005). *Muslims and the state in Britain, France, and Germany*. Cambridge: Cambridge University Press.

Foner, N., & Alba, R. (2008). Immigrant religion in the US and Western Europe: Bridge or barrier to inclusion? *International Migration Review, 42*(2), 360–392.

Fredrickson, G. M. (2002). *Racism: A short history*. Princeton, NJ: Princeton University Press.

Galal Paulsen, L., Liebmann, L. L., & Nordin, M. (2018). Routes and relations in Scandinavian interfaith forums: Governance of religious diversity by states and majority churches. *Social Compass, 65*(3), 329–345.

Gilliat-Ray, S. (2005). From "chapel" to "prayer room": The production, use, and politics of sacred space in public institutions. *Culture and Religion, 6*(2), 287–308.

Glick Schiller, N., & Çağlar, A. (2009). Towards a comparative theory of locality in migration studies: Migrant incorporation and city scale. *Journal of Ethnic and Migration Studies, 35*(2), 177–202.

Goli, M., & Rezaei, S. (2011). Radical Islamism and migrant integration in Denmark: An empirical inquiry. *Journal of Strategic Security, 4*(4), 81–114.

Griera, M., & Nagel, A.-K. (2018). Interreligious relations and governance of religion in Europe: Introduction. *Social Compass, 65*(3), 301–311.

Hoeg, I. M., Kühle, L., Nordin, M., & Christiansen, H. R. (2019). Rooms of silence at three universities in Scandinavia. *Sociology of Religion: A Quarterly Review, 80*(3), 299–322.

Inge, A. (2017). *The making of a Salafi Muslim woman*. Oxford: Oxford University Press.

Iordache, R. E. (2004). The legal status of the Islamic minority in Romania. In R. Aluffi B.-P. and G. Zincone (eds) (Ed.), *The legal treatment of Islamic minorities in Europe*. Leuven: Peeters.

Ipgrave, J., Miller, J., & Hopkins, P. (2010). Responses of three Muslim majority primary schools in England to the Islamic faith of their pupils. *Journal of International Migration & Integration, 11*(1), 73–89.

Jaffe-Walter, R. (2013). "Who would they talk about if we weren't here?" Muslim youth, Liberal schooling, and the politics of concern. *Harvard Educational Review, 83*(4), 613–635.

Kivisto, P. (2014). *Religion and immigration: Migrant faiths in North America and Western Europe*. Malden, MA: Polity.

Kjær, A. M. (2004). *Governance*. London: Polity.

Klinkhammer, G., Frese, H.-L., Satilmis, A., & Seibert, T. (2011). *Interreligiöse und interkulturelle Dialoge mit MuslimInnen in Deutschland: Eine quantitative und qualitative Studie*. Bremen: Bremen University.

References

Körs, A., & Nagel, A.-K. (2018). Local "formulas of peace": Religious diversity and state-interfaith governance in Germany. *Social Compass, 65*(3), 346–362.

Kratochvíl, P., & Doležal, T. (2015). *The European Union and the Catholic Church: Political theology of European integration.* Houndmills, Basingstoke, Hampshire: Palgrave Macmillan.

Linehan, T. (2012). Comparing antisemitism, islamophobia, and Asylophobia: The British case. *Studies in Ethnicity and Nationalism, 12*(2), 366–386.

Lundgren, L. (2021). *A risk or a resource? A study of the Swedish states' shifting perception and handling of minority religious communities between 1952-2019.* PhD Thesis, Ersta Sköndal Bräcke University Collage, Sweden.

Martikainen, T. (2014). Muslim immigrants, public religion and developments towards a post-secular Finnish welfare state. *Tidsskrift for Islamforskning, 8*(1), 78–105.

Martínez-Ariño, J., & Griera, M. (2016). Responses to religious diversity in Spain: Hospitals and prisons from a comparative perspective. *Interdisciplinary Journal for Religion and Transformation in Contemporary Society, 2*(1), 37–59.

Mattes, A., Permoser, J. M., & Stoeckl, K. (2016). Introduction: Institutional responses to religious diversity. *Interdisciplinary Journal for Religion and Transformation in Contemporary Society, 2*(1), 2–11.

Messner, F. (Ed.). (2015). *Public funding of religions in Europe.* Farnham: Ashgate.

Nesser, P. (2015). *Islamist terrorism in Europe: A history.* London: Hurst.

Nexon, D. (2006). Religion, European identity, and political contention in historical perspective. In T. A. Byrnes & P. J. Katzenstein (Eds.), *Religion in an expanding Europe.* Cambridge: Cambridge University Press.

Nielsen, J. S., & Otterbeck, J. (2016). *Muslims in western Europe* (4th ed.). Edinburgh: Edinburgh University Press.

Nordin, M. (2017). Secularization, religious plurality, and position: Local inter-religious cooperation in contemporary Sweden. *Social Compass, 64*(3), 388–403.

Nordin, M. (2018). Blurred religion in contemporary Sweden: Health care institutions as an empirical example. *Journal of Religion in Europe, 11*(2–3), 161–185.

Nordin, M. (2020). How to understand interreligious dialogue in Sweden in relation to the sociocultural context. *Interdisciplinary Journal for Religion and Transformation in Contemporary Society, 6*(2), 429–447.

PREVENT Strategy. (2011). HM Government. June. Cm 8092. https://assets.publishing.service.gov.uk/government/uploads/system/uploads/attachment_data/file/97976/prevent-strategy-review.pdf (Visited 20 August 2021).

Prideaux, M., & Dawson, A. (2018). Interfaith activity and the governance of religious diversity in the United Kingdom. *Social Compass, 65*(3), 363–377.

Rissanen, I. (2012). Teaching Islamic education in Finnish schools: A field of negotiations. In *Teaching and teacher education* (Vol. 28, pp. 740–749).

Romeyn, E. (2014). Anti-Semitism and islamophobia: Spectropolitics and immigration. *Theory, Culture & Society, 31*(6), 77–101.

Rosenow-Williams, K. (2014). Lobbying for civil and religious rights of immigrants and Muslims: Desecuritization strategies of Islamic umbrella organizations in Germany. *Migration & Integration, 15*(3), 411–430.

U.K. Home Office. (2011). *CONTEST: The United Kingdom's Strategy for Countering Terrorism.* July. Cm8123. http://tinyurl.com/5rtjqal (Visited 20 August 2021).

Waldinger, R. (2007). The bounded community: Turning foreigners into Americans in twenty-first century LA. *Ethnic and Racial Studies, 30*(3), 341–374.

Wimmer, A., & Schiller, N. G. (2002). Methodological nationalism and beyond: Nation-state building, migration and the social sciences. *Global Networks, 2*(4), 301–334.

Open Access This chapter is licensed under the terms of the Creative Commons Attribution 4.0 International License (http://creativecommons.org/licenses/by/4.0/), which permits use, sharing, adaptation, distribution and reproduction in any medium or format, as long as you give appropriate credit to the original author(s) and the source, provide a link to the Creative Commons license and indicate if changes were made.

The images or other third party material in this chapter are included in the chapter's Creative Commons license, unless indicated otherwise in a credit line to the material. If material is not included in the chapter's Creative Commons license and your intended use is not permitted by statutory regulation or exceeds the permitted use, you will need to obtain permission directly from the copyright holder.

Part III
Religious Matters

Recently, to calm myself before a show, I have been using Muslim prayer poses in my stretches, and it helps me to feel connected and grounded before getting onstage. When I am in my full Arabian get-up in front of an audience, I sometimes like to sing in Arabic, acting as a vessel for the beautiful queer feminine energies in Islam, feeling the spiritual power of what it means to be queer and to have a room of many different people celebrating this. It is a kind of religious experience, a room united in the celebration of difference; when a show goes really well, it gives me a kind of faith. A faith that Allah's plan was for me to twirl onstage in a skirt so that I could eventually find not only myself, but Allah, like many Sufist Muslims had been doing centuries before me.
    Author Amrou Al-Kadhi
    Unicorn: The Memories of a Muslim Drag Queen by (2019: 282)

The quote above is from a memoir by the drag queen artist Amrou Al-Kadhi who migrated from Bahrain to the UK as a boy. Among other things, the book narrates their (Al-Kadhi prefers this pronoun) long struggle with Islam. In some periods, the faith has repelled Al-Khadi, but from the position they are writing now, as a non-binary adult, they have found the support to embrace their faith in a way than they felt was not on offer when they were younger. Their narrative is about the pressure put on a newly migrated boy wanting to fit in both at school and at home, yet at the same time break free from social shackles. The problem throughout is to identify which protests and positions free Al-Kadhi and which simply tie them down to new contexts with new demands and restrictions. Religion plays a pivotal role. It is a wickedly funny but also painful read. Al-Kadhi's story invites researchers to find new angles and explore the importance of religion for the social, economic and political choices made by migrants. The memoir suggests that we should accept that doubt, periods of intense devotion and the emotions of parents and significant others all shape individual life stories. As we have argued, the religious matters to people's lives, and even migrants who do not identify as religious may be involved indirectly in religious matters by friends and family who engage in religion. Finally, researchers should be aware of that life can be quite queer.

Instead of focusing on the most common questions in migration research that touch upon religion, which were addressed in Part II, Part III emphasises themes that highlight religion in the same way as religious studies, although religious studies are not often connected to migration. Chapter Five discusses the importance of religious acts, roles and ideas about which many migrants care passionately and to which they devote considerable time. Chapter Six summarises by pushing ahead, trying to challenge and invite: to challenge migration research to engage with religion, and to invite new research by identifying some topics that we still need to explore much more fully. Hopefully, the encouragement will spawn new, defiant knowledge and ideas for novel research among readers, be they undergraduate, graduate students, or colleagues. If so, we have achieved the overarching goal of the book.

Reference

Al-Kadhi, A. (2019). *Unicorn: The memories of a Muslim drag queen*. London: 4th Estate.

Chapter 5
Religious Reactions

The themes we have chosen for this chapter are intriguing and complex, and at the same time very specific and typical of contemporary religion, and therefore important when attempting to understand the relation between religion and migration. Others could have been selected. Yet we argue that these themes cover some very dynamic fields. Clearly, some research has been done, however it is our conviction that migration researchers need to engage much more with these themes.

We begin by examining religious practices that are not necessarily formally sanctioned by theology before moving on to discuss migrant missionaries who often have a substantive impact on other migrants. We then turn to conversion as an important process connected to migration and to converts, who frequently play important roles in the religious lives of migrants. This is followed by a focus on the theologies of migrants, including those of migration. Finally, we turn to charity activities and creativity, as these are truly important aspects of the religious ethical and aesthetic values of many migrants.

5.1 Religious Practices

We have argued that religion should be studied as a social phenomenon, as it is upheld by utterances, writings and other actions. It is important to research religiously motivated practices – or habits as they tend to become – as these tend to be crucial for people. Further, practices also connect people to each other and enable the transfer of religion to others, such as younger generations.

Research on migration and religion has focused on these more seemingly private practices to a lesser degree than features such as the public aspects of religion (e.g., Holm Pedersen & Rytter, 2018; Gardner & Grillo, 2002; Dessing, 2001). But religious practices are important for relating the individual and the group to the past, the present and, typically for religion, the future. French sociologist Danièle Hervieu-Léger (2000) describes religion as 'a chain of memory' that creates a sense of awareness of belonging and continuity, with practices functioning as metonyms. Religious practices, supported by religious traditions, may appear to be static – performed in the same manner and to the same extent over long periods of history – and, truly, some practices, not least rituals, have remarkable tenacity over time. However, that is not the whole story; religious practices also change, the legitimation of them changes and the place, time and frequency of where and when they are seen as appropriate change even more often.

Practicing religion also means deciding whether and how to make space and time for it. In Chapter Three (Sects. 3.2.1 and 3.2.2) we introduced the concept 'ritualisation' to emphasise that rituals need to be appropriated by actual people, and when believers position themselves in relation to rituals, when they embody a particular ritual act, they also understand that ritual through their emotions, and through the corporality and the intellectual processing it invites. By default, that appropriation and embodiment become personal. Even central rituals, like the Christian communion, is performed, perceived and understood in different ways depending on the person, but also the place and situation.

It is worth stressing that religious practices do not have to correspond to theological norms; people can perform them with dedication without ever knowing the meaning that religious specialists ascribe to them. Additionally, we would claim that depending on age, life situation and theological knowledge, a single individual will experience the same religious practice in different ways throughout their lives. Not surprisingly, but less often stressed, religious practices after migration tend to find forms acceptable to the surrounding established groups, and quite often new forms develop quickly and take root before religious specialists manage to formulate a legitimation of them through theological thinking (e.g., Dessing et al., 2013; Otterbeck, 2010). Therefore, relations with religious practices should not be presumed in research; they should be studied.

Highlighting religious practices in migration processes also gives us the opportunity to understand more about how gender is negotiated and re-constructed. Gender roles may, for example, be challenged due to new socio-economic patterns. Adult migrant women are to a marked degree engaged in occupational work, younger women pursue higher education and, for many, such patterns tend to coincide with the change in home country, while fewer powerful disciplinary institutions often mean more radical and faster changes. This is not the case, however, for every migrant woman; some will, instead, experience continuity in gender discourses and culturally gendered household chores (e.g., Keaton, 2006; Dessing, 2001; Fortier, 2000; Andizian, 1986). The balance between change and continuity, the expectations of gendered minds and the tenacity of religious discourse and socio-economic conditions are interesting areas of research, especially when combined with gender (e.g., Brah, 1996).

Below, we illustrate three themed trends in religious practices, all partly focusing on gender: the re-conceiving of religion and religious practices over generations; the maintenance of ritual behaviour despite changed gender relations; and finally, the abandoning of religious practice.

5.1.1 *Religious Practices, Generation, and Gender*

Magdalena Nordin (2004) demonstrates that prayers as a religious practice among Swedish-Chileans on an aggregated level seemed to be quite stable, with only minor changes in frequency of prayer due to migration, but this differed on an individual level. One interesting change was location. For some, when still in Chile, prayer mostly took place in a church but in Sweden it was more practiced at home or outdoors in nature. The reason was not a lack of churches, but the way the churches in Sweden affected the Swedish-Chileans – or, rather, did not affect them. As one woman explained, Swedish churches do not 'move me. They do not summon me'. She added that practicing prayer in a church in Sweden is too far removed from who she is; it is not part of her identity (p. 218).

Another example is the wearing of headscarves among Syriac Orthodox Christian immigrants in the European diaspora (Nordin & Westergren, 2023). The practice is strongly gendered and almost exclusively restricted to women, although a few rituals also include headscarves for men. Among Syriac Orthodox churchgoers in Sweden, up to 80 percent of women wear headscarves during the liturgy. However, this practice varies due to occasion, with fewer women wearing it for Christmas, Easter and weddings; timing in the liturgy, with almost every woman wearing it when celebrating Eucharist; and also age, as older women wear large, tight headscarves covering their hair, and younger women use smaller, transparent headscarves. Girls are encouraged in different ways to wear these scarves from a young age, yet there seems to be no demand that they do so; however, for some, not using one was considered a protest against gender discrimination in the church.

In sum, wearing a headscarf appears to be expected, but diversely practiced and slowly changing in the diaspora (Nordin & Westergren, 2023). This is in line with Christine Jacobsen's (2006) study of people active in Muslim youth organisations in Norway in which she demonstrates that negotiations are constantly ongoing and may lead to small shifts in practices, yet there are seldom any clear statements of how things should be or how they should change. What researchers need to be aware of is that even religious behaviour backed up by theological discourse may change quite rapidly with changes social circumstances. Theological discourse is likely to follow rather than lead. On the other hand, social media makes this claim increasingly problematic as behaviour that has manifested itself in discourse in one place may be read and reflected upon in places where similar behaviour has just been initiated. Typically, UK and North American discourses on Islam and gender include some very equal-minded theology that has not been internally produced in Scandinavia until very recently and then often partly inspired by UK and North American discussion and practices (Petersen, 2020). To discover what is truly going on when it comes to changes in religious practices and how theology changes due to this, researchers must actively immerse themselves in observation of religious practice and discussions taking place among religious peers, on social media and at religious gatherings.

5.1.2 Perceiving Religious Practices, but Reimagining Them

Religious practice is often rooted in systems of ideas and behaviour that provides it with context and systemic logic. When socio-economic contexts and social structures have changed due to migration, practices signalling the submission of women might become obsolete but might also be retained and socially renegotiated. For example, Jewish women have traditionally been described as *niddah* (one who is excluded) during menstruation, which means, among other things, that intercourse with a man is prohibited as the woman is in a state of *tumah* (impurity). This state ends after having completed a *mikveh* (ritual bath, lit. a pool of water) 7 days after menstruation finishes. The idea of *niddah* and the importance of the *mikveh* is upheld by some Jewish groups but far from all (Baker, 1993). In North America and the European diaspora, the ritual bath has been reimagined as a spiritual experience rhyming with a more individualised spirituality, while the element of impurity is toned down. Women use the *mikveh* in line with a therapeutic spirituality, as a way of taking control, initiating healing and entering new stages in life (Roos, 2010). Old places for *mikveh* have been revamped and new ones have emerged, taking on the role of spas and rivalling commercial spas. The change seems to have started in the US but has spread worldwide, catering for an era with a changed understanding of the female body and spirituality, yet the reimagined practice still allows the adherents to uphold traditional vocabulary and normative legitimation.

5.1.3 Abandoning Religious Practices

Nora Ahlberg (1991) observed that immigrants from Pakistan to Norway seldom managed to uphold locally grounded practices in the new country; instead, migration brought a new emphasis to theological orthodoxy and orthopraxy. Practices that had been crucial for women's religiosity were abandoned, mainly because they were performed in a sacred geography left behind. Muslim women in Pakistan are not expected to participate in rituals at mosques, and are sometimes hindered from doing so; instead, the country's many shrines, together with other places and objects imbued with the sacred, have been a key element in women's opportunities to engage religiously outside the home. Such localism of religious practice allows the believer to navigate a sacred geography wherein different places can be sought out for different problems and needs, whether health and fertility or fortune and protection from vice (McGuire, 2008: 25). When migration removed believers from the shrines, however, it was difficult to maintain relations with these religious practices.

Pakistani Barelvi Muslims of all genders are involved in regional or local cults, not least around saints. Muslim saints (*pir* in Urdu) are believed to be alive; they transcend the limitations of time and space and can be among the living or simply operating after their earthly existence, meaning they can continue to guide their adherents after migration by sending them dreams and signs in the everyday.

Still, it is at graves or the centres where they operate that the presence of the saints is the strongest. To counter the risk of becoming irrelevant, saints appoint *khalifas* or deputies through whom they work, who bring highly valued greetings, messages or objects that the saint has physically touched into the diaspora; such treasured objects are charged with *baraka*, the spiritual power that flows through the saint. Being close to these objects or understanding the saint's transmitted dreams can be vital for decision making or matters of health, although such extraordinary messages and objects are rare. Clearly, it is a struggle to claim authority and relevance when at a distance; from the adherents' perspective, it seems difficult to uphold practices when separated in space (e.g., Werbner, 2003).

5.2 Missionaries

A particular category of migrants are missionaries who aim to spread and revitalise the message or engage in pastoral care. Many religious organisations are led by persons who have migrated for other reasons, but here we discuss those who travel as missionaries.

The legal situation for missionaries is not the same all over Europe. In most countries, it is legal to proselytise, but in certain countries, notably in eastern Europe, some religions are not recognised and cannot be promoted, especially by foreigners. For example, in Moldova, 'excessive proselytising' is not legal according to Article 4.4 of the Law on Freedom of Conscience, Thought and Religion and foreign citizens are banned from public religious activities if not granted permission by the local authorities. Missionaries from Jehovah's Witnesses and from Pentecostal movements have frequently found themselves discouraged by authorities in states like Bulgaria and Georgia, but also in France where Jehovah's Witnesses in particular have met a lot of resistance over the years (e.g., Besier & Stokłosa, 2016; Byrnes & Katzenstein, 2006).

Below we discuss three examples of migrating missionaries: those who aspire to spread a particular religious interpretation; those who aim to revitalise a faith; and those who come to dispense pastoral care to a parish.

5.2.1 Spreading the Word

In larger western European cities, one is likely to run into migrant missionaries propagating their faith publicly. Christians and Muslims from various groups, the Hare Krishna and Falun Gong activists all take to the streets. Others advertise their faith over the radio or on television or simply at a centre somewhere. One group that stresses mission is the Ahmadiyya Muslim Community whose missionaries can be found all over Europe. Theologically, every Ahmadiyya is seen as a missionary but, practically, only some and only men are trained specifically for the role. The aim is to spread Islam in its Ahmadiyya version through setting examples, *tabligh* (missionary work) and *isha'at* (publications) (Valentine, 2008). Regardless of where they originate, most Ahmadiyya missionaries receive higher religious education in the city of Rabwah, the only Pakistani city where Ahmadiyyas are in the majority. From Rabwah, they are sent to positions all over the world to engage in missionary and pastoral work. The Ahmadiyya scholars are trained in theology, missionary techniques and languages, a training that is then extended to wherever an Ahmadiyya scholar works with a group of adherents. Their publications are translated into local languages as soon as possible, even small languages like those in Nordic countries (Otterbeck, 2000). The movement approaches its work very methodologically.

In 2003 the Ahmadiyya community inaugurated the huge Baitul Futuh Mosque in Morden, south London, which serves as the global headquarters. Apart from being a place of worship, it is also a centre for media production, with the satellite TV channel 'Muslim TV Ahmadiyya International' as one of its main products. The huge centre, an important place for training and networking among the migrating missionaries, attracts Ahmadiyyas to London, thus increasing migration. Part of their missionary strategy is networking. Wherever in Europe you find Ahmadiyyas, they will be attempting to engage in dialogues with established groups of Christians and Jews but rarely with other Muslim groups. The Baitul Futuh mosque is a spacious place for stylish meetings, with great Pakistani food. The Ahmadiyya community invites the highest officials possible – mayors, professors, MPs – to provide the movement with legitimacy and also to create solidarity and security (Valentine, 2008). At the largest meetings, missionaries from all over Europe attend and make certain to bring in important people from the country where they currently live.

When missionaries are working and travelling like this, they generally have good economic backing, contacts and housing. They are educated for the task and might already have learnt the local languages in training. This makes them rather privileged and special among migrants. They are almost exclusively men even though some Protestant missionaries and Buddhist monks are women.

5.2.2 *Revitalizing Faith*

The second group of travelling religious specialists are the revitalisers, preferably charismatics sent by an organisation to invigorate faith. At times, of course, the differences between the first and second group are small or merely depend on perspective.

A powerful narrative circulates among West African charismatic churches that Christianity in Europe is slowly dying. Missionaries are sent to Europe from former colonies to deliver the Christian message back to Europe in so-called reverse mission. This is especially true of Pentecostal groups that actively try to save European souls with a message that is often highly conservative or traditional on questions of gender, sexual preferences and healing. In fact, the movement's message is rather similar to the style of Christianity once presented by colonial powers; indeed, religious practices and beliefs have changed to a lesser degree than in the former colonial centres (e.g., Kubai, 2014; Währisch-Oblau, 2009).

Kim Knibbe (2011) studied the Pentecostal Redeemed Christian Church of God (RCCG), originating in Nigeria, in the Netherlands. To understand the RCCG, transnational, global and colonial power processes must be taken into consideration. The goal of the Church, as for other Pentecostal churches, is to save peoples' souls through Jesus by changing the way they act and think. There are global Pentecostal understandings of what this includes, but, in the case of the RCCG, Knibbe found that they are seen by non-Nigerian citizens as Nigerian (or African) ways to be Christian, whilst among the members of the church they are seen as part of a general Pentecostal way to be Christian. With the goals of reaching out to everyone and re-Christianising Europeans, the RCCG is faced with the delicate task of whether and how to negotiate these fundamental parts of its theology to facilitate these ends (Knibbe, 2011; see also Knibbe, 2018; Pasura, 2014; Ward, 2006).

5.2.3 Pastoral Care

The third group consists of trained religious specialists sent out to provide pastoral care who are regarded by the sending states or organisations as expats. This is an old tradition. Priests, rabbis, monks and imams of different denominations have always travelled with or followed migrants with aspirations of catering to their religious needs in anything from life rituals via prayers to the education of children. Among Muslims, such trained personnel are sent out from Turkey and Morocco, especially targeting people with a Turkish or Moroccan family history. Other states, like Egypt and Saudi Arabia, aspire to reach a broader audience of Arabic speakers but the pattern is same: the state gives salaries to young men who have newly passed their examinations in theology to spend time (often a few years) in Europe (e.g., Nielsen & Otterbeck, 2016). The Turkish Diyanet, the directorate of religious affairs, even offers training in major languages like German for those eager to travel.

Katarina Plank has documented how Theravada Buddhist retreat centres in Sweden are being maintained on the initiative of women born in Thailand who have migrated to Sweden because of marriage (80% of migrants from Thailand to Sweden are women) (Plank et al., 2016; Plank, 2015). These centres invite and provide livelihoods for male monks who uphold and spread sacred knowledge and rituals and provide authority. Generally, the monks have their training in Thai temples and institutions and many of them specifically aim to be able to travel abroad, especially at the beginning of their career; most arrive with a temporary work permit, expecting to return to Thailand eventually. They are generally coordinated by the Thai state and maintain transnational networks with other monks. In many ways, the monks' position is rather precarious as the women have the power to remove them if they are unsatisfied with them, while many of the migrant Theravada Buddhist women have Swedish citizenship – yet another structural advantage. This reverses traditional gendered poles of power and renegotiates religious authority, retaining it in terms of ritual but not guaranteeing that the expected reverence is extended to the young men's social roles. Still, many monks are skilled and liked and there are seldom any problems.

Thus, from the examples above, we can conclude that missionaries and other religious specialists are regarded as crucial by many religious agents. They spread the knowledge of their traditions, engage and enthuse people, generate conversions, have the ambition to school children religiously and publicly represent groups. But they also, to a large extent, fail. They are not very efficient and do not cause mass conversions or engagement. Some have difficulties adapting to new contexts and can be exposed as ignorant about local conditions by second-generation youth who are at home in the context. They are generally better at catering to the first generation's nostalgia than they are at offering paths to those growing up in the diaspora (e.g., Otterbeck, 2010; Jacobsen, 2006).

5.3 Conversions

When trying to understand relations between migration and religion, conversions are important. The research on religious conversion related to migration in western Europe has generally been about conversion to Islam (e.g., Zebiri, 2007; Jensen, 2006; Wohlrab-Sahr, 1999; Köse, 1996), and in a few cases from Islam (e.g., Hassan & Bilici, 2007). The focus has most often been on non-migrant women converting to Islam (e.g., Shanneik, 2012; Soutar, 2010). There are some studies of conversion to Buddhism, not least by Martin Baumann together with a variety of collaborators (e.g., Prebish & Baumann, 2002), but we have encountered little research on conversion to other 'immigrant religions'. We will, however, offer a general presentation of the importance of religious conversion in understanding how migration relates to religion.

5.3.1 What Conversion Can Tell Us About Migration

Conversion raises concern and agitates feelings and, therefore, regularly features in the media in Europe, perhaps suggesting that conversion is a very broad phenomenon; actually, it is numerically marginal. For example, Karagiannis (2011) estimates there to be 200,000 to 320,000 converts to Islam in Europe, making up less than 2 percent of the Muslim population of Europe. Thus, these coverts are less than half a *per mille* of Europe's total population. Hackett et al. (2019) calculate that more people in Europe leave Islam for other religions or for atheism than convert to Islam. Between 2010 and 2016 the net loss was 160,000. Yet, for the people involved – the converts and their partners, children, siblings, parents and friends – it tends to be a lifechanging, deeply emotional experience. In comparison with Islam, the number of converts to Buddhism are estimated in similar absolute figures, but European coverts make up around a third of all Buddhists in Europe (Prebish & Baumann, 2002). Regardless of this difference, both among Muslims and Buddhists, converts are overrepresented among the spokespersons of the respective groups.

Conversion may be part of a refugee's claims to refugee status, prompting the UNHCR (2004) to issue guidelines acknowledging that this is particularly difficult to evaluate and that it comes down to the asylum seeker to prove the gravity of the consequences of conversion in the country of origin and the earnestness of the conversion. Yet if the asylum application is dismissed, an actual conversion may result in imprisonment or even capital punishment in the country of origin. Thus, the authorities responsible for refugee applications have the taxing task of trying to establish whether the conversion is genuine or a tactic to gain asylum, despite the impossibility of finding unbiased ways to measure religious beliefs. Even the religious migrants themselves may have doubts about their own beliefs, are likely to lack formal knowledge of theological propositions and, moreover, are in a very stressful situation. Consequently, there are many cases when religious conversions have not been accepted as sufficient reason to gain refugee status. A 2019 report from the free churches in Sweden showed that 68 percent of the applications by refugees from Afghanistan that made reference to having converted to Christianity were rejected. The decision-making body includes a jury with representatives from the Swedish political parties who exhibit considerable differences in levels of trust. Those from the populist party, the Swedish Democrats, which generally supports an anti-immigration stance, voted in 95 percent of cases to reject such applications, while the Left party's representative – generally supportive of immigration – only proposed that 15 percent should be rejected, a difference of 80 percent (The Conversion Investigation, 2019).

Sometimes immigrants convert to majority churches in the receiving country. In Sweden, the Church of Sweden is one of the religious denominations with the largest number (but not share) of immigrant members, and many of these are converts (Thurfjell & Willander, 2021; see also Mogensen & Damsager, 2007). The Pentecostal churches are generally skilful in attracting immigrant converts. They have a tradition of organising subgroups that follow up on former identities (ex-Muslims for example) and cater to minority languages (Nordin, 2004, 2007). Are these conversions also processes of integration? While it is apparent that immigrants can be integrated into religious groups, that does not automatically lead to integration into the wider society. In European countries, religious belonging is not necessarily a bridge to inclusion. In fact, it may be the other way around, regardless of whether the belonging is to a Pentecostal or a majority church. Nonetheless, for the individual, turning to the right religious group might be invaluable, as it may lead to job opportunities, future partners and, evidently, ontological security.

Conversion often involves marriage. In most religions, the religious scholars promote marriage with co-religionists but may still tolerate marriage to spouses of other religions. Undoubtedly, some convert to enable marriage and it is difficult to judge from the outside if conversion is due to conviction or a tactic. Marriages outside one's own ethno-religious group can be seen as an important part of the integration processes, as was pointed out by US researcher Milton Gordon (1964) over half a century ago. After the initial establishment of a new religious group through migration, the next generation tends to marry people from other migrant and established groups, either respecting religious convention or not depending on the flexibility of religious dogmas, which range from tolerant to downright condemnatory.

5.3.2 Conversion and Identity

Identity formation in the processes of conversion has been a major theme in research on the phenomenon. Lewis Rambo (1993) has constructed an influential theory in which the importance of both context and time is crucial. Context is to be understood both at a micro (life history) and macro (society) level and needs to include social, cultural, religious and personal aspects. The conversion process (time) includes the initial crisis and quests, and later encounters, interactions, commitments and consequences, all of which have varying degrees of salience and insignificance during the conversion process.

These aspects are also part of the processes that people in Europe undergo when converting to Islam (e.g., Shanneik, 2012; Köse, 1999; Sultán, 1999; Wohlrab-Sahr, 1999). In her research on Danes – both men and women – converting to Islam, Tina Jensen (2006) highlights the different ways of being Muslim among these converts on the long and winding road leading to Islam, and how this process continues even after the formal ritual of conversion has taken place. For the Danish converts there is an ongoing negotiation between adoption by Muslim communities, communities constructed among Danish converts, former religious belongings and society in general. Among the Danish converts in this study, only 52 percent had resigned their membership in the Danish Folk Church and their new Muslim names were seldom registered.

Yafa Shanneik found many similar processes of identity formation in her study of young women in Ireland converting to Islam (2012). She highlights these women's own agency in the conversion process, and notes that their view of Catholicism helps motivate the conversion due to their perceptions of their greater opportunities for status and power in Islam than in 'post-Catholic' society in general. As Shanneik writes, 'Their conversion is a space that offers women, to a certain extent, autonomy as well as social and religious status—a kind of empowerment they did not have before becoming Muslims' (Shanneik, 2012: 167). Shanneik also shows that, while the conversion processes are driven by their own agency, they are also under the control of the Muslim communities they join.

In their study in 2007, Mogensen and Damsager reflected on whether conversions related to immigration can change the very idea of Danishness. If people change their religious belonging – for example, immigrants to the Danish Folk Church and non-immigrants ('ethnic Danes') to Islam, Buddhism or Hinduism – is it then, over time, reasonable to construct a national Danish identity that includes belonging to the Danish Folk Church? Growing religious pluralism and an interplay between religious belonging and immigrant / non-immigrant background is to be considered when trying to answer that question (Mogensen & Damsager, 2007).

5.4 New Theologies

First, a note on our use of the term theology. A strict understanding reserves it for writings addressing how adherents are to understand the transcendent reality assumed by their beliefs. Yet today, the term is also used as an umbrella concept covering the devout ideas held in a religious discourse by the adherents – sometimes reserved for the religious specialists, sometimes applied more liberally to include all believers' beliefs. Of course, the word also labels an academic discipline. Below, we connect to the broader use of the word. We do not reserve the concept for Christianity.

In most places, theology as a discipline is a product that is strategically cultivated through meticulously crafted educational career paths and monitored by religious authorities. The most dominant theologies tend to have the institutional and legal support of states and their influence may be reflected in a broad range of phenomena such as religious education in schools, the ordering of time (the working week, which days are holidays) and what is allowed to be said or done in public (blasphemy laws).

The theologies of European minorities, formed through recent migration, are not powerfully monitored, as their institutions are rarely as developed as those of established groups. Does migration then generate opportunities for unbridled thinking in theology? Yes, potentially, but not automatically. When migrants end up in a place where the religion of birth or choice is not as monitored and disciplined, there are, potentially, opportunities to develop new impulses or expand on previously curbed ideas. At the least, these attempts are harder to control. Social media has further created a situation where it is much easier to reach out and find people sympathetic to novel ideas or to find new interpretations in the first place. There is no shortage of examples of innovative thinking after migration (e.g., Hashas, 2019; Hoover & Clark, 2002) but also of cases of migrants who form tightknit groups in new environments and have rather increased compliance within the group, although there is a lack of studies focusing on sectarianism or isolationist strategies among religious migrations to Europe. Below, we address four main forms of new theologies: liberal, revivalist, conservative and theologies of migration.

5.4.1 Liberal Theologies

When new, so-called liberal or progressive theologies are being formulated by immigrants to Europe, typically, the big questions of the day are addressed: ecology and the environment, pluralism in faiths or co-existence with other faiths, social and gender equality or equity if called for, human rights, animal rights, vegetarianism or veganism and sexual and gender pluralism. Individual empowerment and ethics tend to be at the heart of solutions. Often, inspiration – openly, with literature references – is found in the work of European and North American philosophers, social critics and theologians from other religions or among co-religionists who have already become part of global discourses on empowerment and ethics. Books are regularly published by European and North American university presses or established publishers and marketed in the same way as other books of the same genre. For example, when looking for LBGTQIA+-friendly theology within Islam, regardless of language, you tend to find the most progressive, affirmative books, internet sites and organisations in Europe and North America, where, admittedly, some of the main actors are converts, not migrants. Regardless, most of these work closely with migrants and draw from their experiences (e.g., Shah, 2018; Kugle, 2014). It is an open question how this plays out in different religious environments, but researchers can be rather certain that there are reactions brewing.

By framing new liberal theologies as individual empowerment and ethics we are highlighting crucial structures if not the full picture. The individual empowerment discourse is a key development in the history of ideas, covering the empowerment and legal protection (and creating the ideal) of the citizen and the vote, followed by empowerment of women, children, ethnic, 'racial' and religious minorities and sexual minorities. Just as these empowerment ideas have affected laws in many states (to various degrees), they have affected religious thought too. Does migration play a role in this?

The ideal of human rights, and international agreements supporting such ideals, has put formidable pressure on religious traditions to address norms and values that are perceived to conflict with them; in effect, human rights ideals compete with other ethical codes like religious traditions (Ferrari, 2021), and rights to divorce, equal rights in marriage and the right to change religion, among others, may provoke reactions. At the same time, human rights promote both individual and collective religious freedom, within limits, and may secure the chance for religious migrants to practice and preach in their new home countries. Still, in many cases, the same discourses also allow for new interpretations in former home countries. There are global flows of theological trends that affect interpretations and practices worldwide, not only among migrants (Otterbeck, 2000). One can also observe how transnational connections contribute to the exchange of ideas.

5.4.2 Revivalist Theologies

The typical trait of revivalist theology is the bypassing of history and a so-called return to the sources. Generally, revivalist theologies overlap with liberal theology, but also with conservatism. They tend to be in tension with late modernity, while paralleling certain traits from modernist social movements and often nurturing a millennial or messianic spirit. Some revivalist theology gets enmeshed in sectarian environments; other versions are personal projects (e.g., Marty & Scott Appleby, 1995).

In migration, the turn to revivalist theology may be facilitated by the lack of institutional plausibility structures disciplining interpretation and insisting on continuity with tradition; new structures and authorities may emerge. When Muslim immigration to Europe increased from the mid-1980s, for example, a combination of Arabic Muslim Brotherhood, Pakistani Jamaat-i Islami and Saudi Wahhabi theology circulated in immigrant circles. Preachers were often engineers, teachers and medical doctors – people with higher education but not in religious studies – who laid the foundation of Islamic organisations all over Europe, pushing a revivalist agenda that alienated many Muslims (e.g., Roy, 2004; Otterbeck, 2000; Kepel, 1987). The theology clearly challenged traditional authority, blaming it for obstructing the expansion of Islam; however, it also resulted in some of the most profiled thinkers of this type moving to live and develop their thoughts in Europe and North America. Organisations like the Islamic Foundation in the UK (e.g., Janson, 2002) or the International Institute for Islamic Thought in the USA (e.g., Stenberg, 1996) thrived in the diaspora, free from the repression of state apparatuses fearing their message.

Another common phenomenon is that revivalist movements in the home country are supported from the diaspora. When the Hindutva movements grew in India it had both intellectual and economic support from Hindus in Europe and, interestingly, while the religio-political agenda in relation to India is strong, the main feature and function in Europe is a strong religio-cultural chauvinism. Pride and rigorous Hindu lifestyles are promoted in both soft and hard neo-Hindutva forms, which range from focusing on a Hindu religio-cultural alternative to promoting and attempting to monitor Hindu practice and faith of a particular kind (e.g., Sengupta & Swamy, 2020).

Thus, when researching migration and religion, revivalist theology may be a very crucial aspect of phenomena as different as economic and political activities, and ethnic and cultural identities and meaning making. Simply put, the investment in a particular theology may explain migrants' priorities.

5.4.3 Conservative Theologies

In western European, conservative theologies are frequently portrayed as the antithesis of post/late modernity and, thus, undesirable. Conservatism in religion may in fact be one of the major reasons why many citizens consider religion something alien because those attracted to conservative theologies are the most distanced from the ideals of post/late-modern society (e.g., Aydemir, 2012; Bracke, 2012). The prevalence of conservative theologies suggests negotiations that did not lead to change, or possibly that changes included codifying or seeking to explore earlier manifestations of a religion, which aligns conservatism with revivalism. Conservative theologies seek to legitimise religion – practices, theologies, morals and ethics – in a new setting, often by claiming a particular form to be historically authentic. Generally, compared to modernism that looks at how to improve things in future, conservative theologies look back to periods understood to have better morals, ethics and religious discipline.

But let us challenge the seemingly static appearance of conservative theologies. When a religion is brought to another place by migrants, it tends to lead to negotiations over practices and reflections about theology. There is ongoing interplay among migrants between merely living the religion, relating to religious scriptures and perceptions that the authority of religious specialists and institutions legitimises religious interpretations. Conservative theologies appeal to many migrants as they suggest continuity in faith. Rituals and morals, but also aesthetics in decoration, language and clothing – to give a few examples – may acquire symbolic value, proof of the survival of the religious community in times of change. The alternative – innovation and modification – may be conceived of as a riskier course forced upon a community in a new setting (e.g., Mayer, 2014; Dessing, 2001). Thus, upholding conservatism, the culture and traditions, as well as religious traditions linked to the country of origin, requires continuous work and choices, and often it is impossible or meaningless to try to separate culture from religious ideas, although theologies are of another order as they are verbalised and very often have institutional backing (Röder, 2014). It is therefore crucial to understand conservative theologies, how they are voiced in a group (in the family, by religious specialists and peers) and their importance to life choices regarding more mundane aspects like careers, gender roles, education and finances.

5.4.4 Theologies of Migration

Another reaction to migration is to create further theology on the topic or clarify the theology about it, causing intellectuals and religious specialists to revisit the importance of migration, relations with the stranger and the implications of pluralism in their respective traditions. Such discussions are highly important in European churches in connection with ideals about the ethical duty to protect the stranger – or in many cases the refugee – from unfair treatment, resulting in cases of Christian parishes, pastors or priests hiding asylum seekers (regardless of religion) from the authorities and the police when they consider deportation unfair. The ethics of giving shelter to the stranger has a long history in Abrahamic religions as well as Hinduism and Buddhism and this has been brought to the fore by important voices, often in conflict with states and at times their own religious organisations (Collier & Strain, 2014).

Reflections on the migrant and migration tend to connect to philosophical and psychological writing on the role of the stranger in our mental categories, discussion about human rights and the central myths, foundation texts and theological explications of various traditions (Collier & Strain, 2014). Organisations formed by migrants and individuals with a recent migration history may conform with these ethics and many go out of their way to help, while religious world leaders from the Dalai Lama to the Catholic Pope address the issue in widely disseminated public speeches. While hate speech is carefully studied, less attention has been paid to discourses among the religious of ethical responsibility, subsuming charity (see Sect. 5.4) and interfaith dialogue (see Sect. 4.3) in relation to migration to Europe.

A theology of migration of a less liberal kind can be found in the reformulation of migration as *da'wa*, the calling to people to engage in Islam. Classically, it was not recommended in Muslim theology to settle in lands dominated by non-Muslims. Travelling, visiting, even residing for periods was accepted if one could perform the basics of one's religion, but not permanent settlement. Because of the numerically large migration to countries dominated by non-Muslims after World War II, theologians, especially Pakistanis from Jamaat-i Islam, tried to legitimise it by creating a new understanding of *da'wa*. The legitimacy of settling in Europe was conditional on migrants setting good examples by living Islamically moral lives and showing kindness and patience to others – the equivalent of calling to Islam through words, which is the expected activity of someone doing *da'wa*. This notion of *da'wa* by example was spread in numerous speeches and pamphlets in Urdu, English and other languages from the 1980s and onwards (e.g., Janson, 2002; Poston, 1992).

A final theology of migration is the idea of missionary migration, the merit of participating in missionary work, prominently nurtured by the Mormon Church but also several Pentecostal churches (see Sect. 5.6). Ultimately, the decision to migrate may actually be based on an understanding of what God requires from you.

5.5 Charity

Economic and material aid is needed by troubled people all over the world, but to migrants who have secured a job and a home in a new country sharing is often not only seen as a decent thing to do but a religious duty. People engage in what Peggy Levitt (2008: 772) calls 'theologies of change about how to make the world a better place'. An abundance of charity organisations are motivated by a religious ethos, many of which are initiated by migrants.

5.5.1 Migrants' NGO Religious Charities

Apart from a few studies, research on charity organisations set up by migrants and the reasoning behind their engagement is scarce (e.g., Erdal & Borgchgrevink, 2016; Juul Petersen, 2015), yet migrants involved in religious charity work organise charity concerts, aid giving, soup kitchens, women's shelters and poverty relief initiatives. These religious initiative-takers make space in Europe, advertising their activities and asking for donations on the streets, and contributions of food, clothes, books and other goods for redistribution at collection points labelled with their names and logos.

The world's second largest Muslim NGO, Islamic Relief, was founded in the UK in 1984 by migrants, along with Human Appeal (formed 1991), Muslim Hands (1993), Muslim Charity (1999), Islamic Aid (2000), Penny Appeal (2009) and many more. In the stories of their respective origins, there are two recurring components: personal migration narratives and being awoken to global crises by events like the genocide in Bosnia. Several, likely all, large Muslim organisations, such as the Ahmadiyya Muslim Association UK, also participate in charity work, while many mosques gather or channel gifts. Typical activities include sponsoring the building of welfare institutions like schools and hospitals or donating to religious causes by building mosques or providing religious education. At times, donations are made to catastrophe areas and religio-political movements (Juul Petersen, 2015).

Immigrants to Europe and North America also engage in charity projects in former home regions. Today, researchers in medical anthropology are sensitive to the need to decolonialise the expectations of aid provision to make it more efficient and less intrusive, something Aneel Singh Brar et al. (2021) reflect upon when analysing a maternal health initiative taken by Canadian Sikh health science professionals in a North Indian Sikh context. They note that charity from emigrants – who are aware of cultural habits and values and are sensitised to development in former home countries or regions – is generally less intertwined with politics or missionary ambitions than the charity supplied by states and some charity organisations. On the other hand, emigrants may come from families that are privileged in the former home countries and their projects may cement social hierarchies. They may even be framed by saviour narratives in which the emigrant brings the culture, values and medical knowledge of 'the West' to the 'underdeveloped' country of origin. To be successful, the balance between different cultural understandings of health must be considered, as not all help may be welcome (Brar et al., 2021). Ethnicity, class, gender and politics, as well as religious affiliation or type of faith, might all be reasons not to accept charity.

5.5.2 *The Importance of Economic Remittances*

Not only organisations act, individuals also contribute, giving to church collections for the aid of victims of earthquakes, famines and the like. Other migrants remain close to a religious organisation in the former home country, donating, paying membership fees or even different forms of tithe or *khums*, depending on religion. This again emphasises the importance of transnational religious ties in the world of migrants. Religious convictions and group belonging have the potential to form tremendously resilient bonds (e.g., Werbner, 2003; Levitt, 2001).

Giving, supporting and making a difference are important ways to accentuate notions of both individual and collective (religious) ethics and good citizenship. As a female Muslim informant in Levitt's study on civic engagement (2008: 782) says, 'When we help anyone, besides just our own, we set an example of how to

5.6 Creativity in the Arts 105

change the world.' The ability to provide economic remittances after migration is not only a possibility but, to many, a moral obligation often informed by a complex web of moral orders, religion being one of them. Fulfilling the role of male breadwinner and provider, for example, is deeply ingrained in gendered expectations partly informed by religion. Obviously, women migrants, individually or as part of a family, also provide economic remittances to family, relatives or aid projects but men who adhere to strongly patriarchal traditions seem to feel a special pressure to provide and feelings of failure if unable to do so (e.g., Stevanovic, 2012; Thai, 2006).

Migrants among the super-rich can act with impressive impact and donate whole buildings or infrastructural projects, and set up funds, endowments or stipends to help others develop. While there is little or no research on this, the information below is taken from widespread reports in the mass media. For example, FC Barcelona Femení's striker, Asisat Oshoala, is a Nigerian, Yoruba Muslim, open about believing in God and praying. In 2019, she set up the Asisat Oshoala Foundation with the specific aim of empowering women's football in Nigeria, including the hijab project, launched in March 2022,[1] that aims to enable Muslim girls to take part. A specially designed hijab was provided, allowing teenage Muslim girls to acknowledge religious moral guidelines while playing. Likewise, several migrants among English Premier League's male footballers give generously to regions where they grew up, sometimes mentioning religious obligations as the main motivator. Among them is Crystal Palace's Wilfried Zaha, who has given 10 percent of his salary to Ivory Coast charities and an orphanage throughout his career. Giving a tithe is a well-established Christian tradition and Zaha, who is public about his Christian beliefs, states in interviews that it is a chance to help given by God.

The research on economic remittances sent by migrants is vast and so is the impact of these. Religiously motivated donors and religious charities are somewhat less studied. Often, religion is mentioned as a giver's motivation, but it is rare to find detailed analysis of the religious component, its importance or the role played by religious organisations and celebrities as role models.

5.6 Creativity in the Arts

As migration is generally a life changing experience, whether travelling as a privileged migrant or an irregular migrant without the required papers, some migrants channel their emotions, thoughts and reactions through creative expression (Gonçalves & Majhanovich, 2016) and religion may play a part, directly or indirectly. It is an important field of research, if unpredictable, as individual experiences and motives become part of the art (Illman, 2014). Studies of such works have a rich, exciting, naturally occurring data source. Below, we describe four fields: art

---

[1] https://www.instagram.com/p/CbNCIdmgsad. Visited 6 April 2002.

that is critical of religious expression in former or new homelands; art that is nostalgic or celebratory – in form and content – in relation to religious arts in former homelands; those that use popular art expressions in the new homelands to affirm religion; and finally art meant for dialogue. Evidently, at times, these trends overlap.

5.6.1 Art Critical of Religious Expressions in Former Homelands

Censorship, self-censorship and consideration of the feelings and safety of oneself and others is a common hindrance to expressing critique against religion. Severe censorship laws like those in Pakistan, supervising governmental censorship bodies as in Thailand or Iran or the power of organised religion over public spheres exemplified in Russia or Egypt are not to be taken lightly (Kirkegaard et al., 2017). In a migration setting, critique may flourish. Admittedly, prior to the growth of the Internet this was easier and less risky. Today, governments use search engines to pursue the transgressive history of individuals; indeed, artists might be held accountable for criticism expressed during a period when it was safer to do so (Kirkegaard, 2017).

Criticism of religion often targets gender inequalities and the corruption of religious leaders but may also be specifically directed at religious dogma. Using symbols and narratives normally treated piously, artists take swings against religions with different degrees of sophistication. In a social scientific analysis of migration and religion, it is rarely enough only to interpret the artwork itself, more nuance is gained if researchers also interview the creator(s) and investigate its reception, as many migrants have emotionally scarring experiences of injustice and a political drive to work against those they hold responsible.

The impact of the art produced by diasporic communities is sometimes huge. Reactions to sections of Salman Rushdie's novel *The Satanic Verses* (1988), for example, changed things on a personal level for the author – a migrant from India to the UK– forcing him into hiding, exposing him to violence, but also on a much larger scale. The novel contained direct criticism of Ayatollah Khomeini and the credulity of Indian popular religiosity but, most importantly, it featured a drastic reimagining of the foundational history of Islam (with the aim to criticise historical negative attitudes towards Islam, as well as racism in the UK in 1980s). Political relations between Iran and the UK deteriorated and the populist political imagination in Europe increasingly came to target Muslims, positioning them as cultural others incompatible with European civilisation and norms (e.g., Nielsen & Otterbeck, 2016). The novel caused Muslim citizens in Britain to participate in protests in the public sphere as Muslims, a trend that has continued to grow, and also divided them. While Rushdie had not respected traditional sensibilities, no one could have foreseen the events that followed; reactions to his novel became a game changer.

5.6.2 Art that Is Nostalgic or Celebratory in Relation to Religious Arts in Former Homelands

A less controversial style is religious art aiming to reproduce established religious form and content. Heritage and nostalgia play an important part in this, not least when decorating rooms and buildings where migrants gather for prayer and other religious practices. Decorations, calligraphy, images and at least some architectural features should preferably be crafted in distinct ways, often requiring skills well beyond the amateur. Music might be necessary, which may require special instruments, musical technique or architectural features to reproduce the preferred sound texture. Is a music file an option or is a live performance preferred or required, even if on a basic skills level? Further, art carries connotations, some easy to decipher, others more esoteric and less known. Some take a stand against traditional mysticism that tends to be interlaced with traditional arts, to the level that many believers hardly perceive mysticism as separate but, rather, as an integrated and necessary part of artistic expression. This is as clear in Christian psalms as in Sufi poetry. People tend to be passionate about art and studying conflict over artistic expression in a religious environment formed by migrants may provide valuable illustration of different religious trends (Otterbeck, 2021).

Some migrants spend both time and money learning traditional skills, not least on an amateur level. Courses are arranged on how to make a mandala, perform a sacred dance or paint an icon, and people travel far to hone their skills with masters of a tradition, some of whom are themselves migrants, bringing their skills as musicians, poets and calligraphists with them to make a living in the new context, both performing and guiding others. Such cultural capital may prove very important both for the individual's finances and also for migrants sharing an aesthetic tradition (DiMaggio & Fernández-Kelly, 2010).

5.6.3 Arts that Use Popular Art Expressions in the New Homelands to Affirm Religion

Increasing numbers of migrants affirm their religions through the dominant and popular forms of creative expression in new homelands, especially migrants who arrived as children and have grown up listening to both the music from a prior homeland and the popular music of their generation. Lebanese-Swedish singer, songwriter, performer, and producer Maher Zain is deeply involved with his Muslim faith. Hugely popular worldwide among Muslims, his songs embrace different styles – pop-reggae, RnB, Arabic pop, ballads. The lyrics to his songs are deeply devout. Otterbeck (2021) has observed how important religious ethics are for such artists: the art, the artist's persona and what is visible of the private person must resonate with religious norms to enable the artist to come across as authentic. For global artists like Maher Zain this becomes a particular challenge, as they cannot please everyone all the time. Yet, these artists, novelists and actors are claimed and cherished, often with ethno-religious pride.

Creative expressions are also used to address racism, discrimination and prejudice in new home countries. Narrative genres of the arts are used to debate, illustrate and target Islamophobia, antisemitism and Christophobia. Novels, films, lyrics, comics, graffiti and poetry all lend form to creative expressions countering stereotypes and calling for change (Martiniello, 2019).

Very successful artists and craftspeople are often mobile and travel the world, speaking from positions of influence, and those who are devout carry their religious beliefs and practices with them for all to see. Some studies focus on the artists and their art, but researchers would also do well to study the reception or the appropriation of it by the audience and consumers.

5.6.4 Arts for Dialogue

An interesting field of research is what Ruth Illman (2014) calls creative interreligious dialogue, meaning the contribution of creative artists to dialogue, some of them migrants. Illman has studied the efforts of six artists to create in-depth understanding in line with Martin Buber's dialogue philosophy, which calls for acknowledgment of the 'similarity-in-difference' of the other, resulting in art that passionately pleas for recognition or challenges to normality.

Another field is so-called participatory projects where migrants from impoverished areas might participate in making art (often music or photography). Usually such projects are initiated by the established (municipalities, researchers, politicians) with the hope of creating inclusion and dialogue. Other top-down forums are museums that use religious art and artefacts to initiate cultural dialogue; however, while art engages, research has shown that results are difficult to control or evaluate. In fact, when approached in an instrumental way, ambitions often fail (e.g., Wilson, 2017; Johansson, 2015).

References

Ahlberg, N. (1991). Muslimska kvinnor i migrationsperspektiv. In N. G. Holm (Ed.), *Islam i forskningens ljus* (pp. 183–213). Åbo: Åbo akademi.

Andizian, S. (1986). Women's roles in organizing symbolic life: Algerian female immigrants in France. In R. J. Simon & C. B. Brettell (Eds.), *International migration: The female experience* (pp. 254–266). New Jersey: Rowman & Allanheld.

Aydemir, M. (2012). Dutch Homonationalism and intersectionality. In E. Boehmer & S. De Mul (Eds.), *The postcolonial low countries: Literature, colonialism, and multiculturalism* (pp. 178–202). Lanham, MD: Lexington Press.

References

Baker, A. (1993). *The Jewish women in contemporary society: Transitions and traditions.* Houndsmills: Macmillan.
Besier, G., & Stokłosa, K. (Eds.). (2016). *Jehovah's witnesses in Europe: Past and present volume 1.* Newcastle: Cambridge Scolars Press.
Bracke, S. (2012). From "saving women" to "saving gays": Rescue narratives and their dis/continuities. *European Journal of Women's Studies, 19*(2), 237–252.
Brah, A. (1996). *Cartographies of diaspora: Contesting identities.* London: Routledge.
Brar, A. S., Hedt-Gauthier, B. L., & Hirschhorn, L. R. (2021). Mixed methods lot quality assurance sampling: A novel rapid methodology to inform equity focused maternal health programming in rural Rajasthan, India. *PLoS One,* online published 29 April.
Byrnes, T. A., & Katzenstein, P. J. (Eds.). (2006). *Religion in an expanding Europe.* Cambridge: Cambridge University Press.
Collier, E. W., & Strain, C. R. (Eds.). (2014). *Religious and ethical perspectives on global migration.* Lanham: Lexington.
Dessing, N. M. (2001). *Rituals of birth, circumcision, marriage, and death among Muslims in The Netherlands.* Leuven: Peeters.
Dessing, N. M., Jeldtoft, N., Nielsen, J., & Woodhead, L. (Eds.). (2013). *Everyday lived Islam in Europe.* Farnham: Ashgate.
DiMaggio, P., & Fernández-Kelly, P. (Eds.). (2010). *Art in the lives of immigrant communities in the United States.* New Brunswick, NJ: Rutgers University Press.
Erdal, M. B., & Borgchgrevink, K. (2016). Transnational Islamic charity as everyday rituals. *Global Networks, 17*(1), 130–146.
Ferrari, S. (2021). Rights of man, rights of god: An unavoidable tension? *Religion & Human Rights, 15*(3), 241–255.
Fortier, A.-M. (2000). *Migrant belongings: Memory, space and identity.* Oxford: Berg Publisher.
Gardner, K., & Grillo, R. (2002). Transnational households and ritual: An overview. *Global Networks, 2*(3), 179–190.
Gonçalves, S., & Majhanovich, S. (Eds.). (2016). *Art and intercultural dialogue.* Sense Publishers.
Gordon, M. M. (1964). *Assimilation in American life: The role of race, religion, and national origins.* New York: Oxford University Press.
Hackett, C., Stonawski, M., Potančoková, M., Connor, P., Shi, A. F., Kramer, S., & Marshall, J. (2019). Projections of Europe's growing Muslim population under three migration scenarios. *Journal of Religion and Demography, 6*(1), 87–122.
Hashas, M. (2019). *The idea of European Islam: Religion, ethics, politics and perpetual modernity.* London: Routledge.
Hassan, K. M., & Bilici, M. (2007). Conversion out of Islam: A study of conversion narratives of former Muslims. *The Muslim World, 97*(1), 111–124.
Hervieu-Léger, D. (2000). *Religion as a chain of memory.* New Brunswick, NJ: Rutgers University Press.
Holm Pedersen, M., & Rytter, M. (2018). Rituals of migration: An introduction. *Journal of Ethnic and Migration Studies, 44*(16), 2603–2616.
Hoover, S., & Clark, L. S. (Eds.). (2002). *Practicing religion in the age of the media: Explorations in media, religion, and culture.* New York: Columbia University Press.
Illman, R. (2014). *Art and belief: Artists engaged in interreligious dialogue.* London: Routledge.
Jacobsen, C. M. (2006). *Staying on the straight path: Religious identities and practices among young Muslims in Norway.* PhD Thesis, University of Bergen, Norway.
Janson, T. (2002). *Invitation to Islam: A history of Da'wa.* Stockholm: Swedish Science Press.
Jensen, T. (2006). Religious authority and autonomy intertwined: The case of converts to Islam in Denmark. *The Muslim World, 96*(4), 643–660.
Johansson, C. (2015). *Museums, migration and cultural diversity: Swedish museums in tune with the times?* Innsbruck: Studien Verlag.
Juul Petersen, M. (2015). *For humanity or for the Umma? Aid and Islam in transnational Muslim NGOs.* London: Hurst & Company.

Karagiannis, E. (2011). Islamic activism in Europe: The role of converts. *CTC Sentinel, 4*(8), 16–19. August.
Keaton, T. D. (2006). *Muslim girls and the other France: Race, identity politics, & social exclusion*. Bloomington: Indiana University Press.
Kepel, G. (1987). *Les Banlieues de l'Islam*. Paris: Editions du Seui I.
Kirkegaard, A. (2017). Silencing artists: Reflections on music censorship in the case of Mahsa Vahdat. In A. Kirkegaard, H. Järviluoma, J. S. Knudsen, & J. Otterbeck (Eds.), *Researching music censorship*. Newcastle upon Tyne: Cambridge Scholars Publishing.
Kirkegaard, A., Järviluoma, H., Knudsen, J. S., & Otterbeck, J. (Eds.). (2017). *Researching music censorship*. Newcastle upon Tyne: Cambridge Scholars Publishing.
Knibbe, K. E. (2011). Nigerian missionaries in Europe: History repeating itself or a meeting of modernities. *Journal of Religion in Europe, 4*(3), 471–487.
Knibbe, K. E. (2018). Secularist understandings of Pentecostal healing practices in Amsterdam: Developing an intersectional and post-secularist sociology of religion. *Social Compass, 65*(5), 650–666.
Köse, A. (1996). *Conversion to Islam: A study of native British converts*. London: Kegan Paul.
Köse, A. (1999). The journey from the secular to the sacred: Experiences of native British converts to Islam. *Social Compass, 46*(3), 301–312.
Kubai, A. (2014). Accommodation and tension: African Christian communities and their Swedish hosts. In H. Vilança, E. Pace, I. Furseth, & P. Pettersson (Eds.), *The changing soul of Europe: Religions and migrations in Northern and Southern Europe* (pp. 149–172). Farnham: Ashgate.
Kugle, S. S. al-H. (2014). *Living out Islam: Voices of gay, lesbian, and transgender Muslims*. New York: New York University Press.
Levitt, P. (2001). *The transnational villagers*. Berkeley: University of California Press.
Levitt, P. (2008). Religion as path to civic engagement. *Ethnic and Racial Studies, 31*(4), 766–791.
Martiniello, M. (2019). Immigrants, refugees and the arts: A complex and multidimensional relationship. In B. Dogramaci & B. Mersmann (Eds.), *Handbook of art and global migration: Theories, practices, and challenges* (pp. 70–75). Berlin: De Gruyter.
Marty, M. E., & Scott Appleby, R. (Eds.). (1995). *Fundamentalisms comprehended* (The fundamentalism project vol. 5). Chicago: Chicago University Press.
Mayer, J.-F. (2014). "We are Westerners and must remain Westerns": Orthodoxy and Western rites in Western Europe. In M. Hämmerli & J.-F. Mayer (Eds.), *Orthodox identities in Western Europe: Migration, settlement and innovation* (pp. 267–289). London: Routledge.
McGuire, M. B. (2008). *Lived religion: Faith and practice in everyday life*. Oxford: Oxford University Press.
Mogensen, M. S., & Damsager, J. H. M. (Eds.). (2007). *Dansk konversionsforskning*. Højbjerg: Forlaget Univers.
Nielsen, J. S., & Otterbeck, J. (2016). *Muslims in western Europe* (4th ed.). Edinburgh: Edinburgh University Press.
Nordin, M. (2004). *Religiositet bland migranter: Sverige-chilenares förhållande till religion och samfund*. Lund: Centre for Theology and Religious Studies.
Nordin, M. (2007). Immigrant language groups in religious organisations. *Nordic Journal of Religion and Society, 1*(20), 65–86.
Nordin, M., & Westergren, A. (2023). Veiled integration: The use of headscarves among a Christian minority in Sweden. *International Journal of Religion, 4*(3), 3–18.
Otterbeck, J. (2000). *Islam på svenska: Tidskriften Salaam och islams globalisering*. Stockholm: Almqvist & Wiksell.
Otterbeck, J. (2010). *Samtidsislam: Unga muslimer i Malmö och Köpenhamn*. Stockholm: Carlsson.
Otterbeck, J. (2021). *The awakening of Islamic pop music*. Edinburgh: Edinburgh University Press.
Pasura, D. (2014). *African transnational diasporas: Fractured communities and plural identities of Zimbabweans in Britain*. Basingstoke: Palgrave Macmillan.
Petersen, J. (2020). *The making of a mosque with female imams: Serendipities, structures, and framing of Islam in Denmark*. Lund: Lund University.

References

Plank, K. (2015). The sacred foodscapes of Thai Buddhist temples in Sweden. *Scripta Instituti Donneriani Aboensis, 26*, 201–224.

Plank, K., Raddock, E., & Selander, P. (2016). The Temple Mount of Fredrika: Translocality and fractured transnationalism of a visionary Thai Buddhist retreat centre. *Contemporary Buddhism, 17*(2), 405–426.

Poston, L. (1992). *Islamic Da'wah in the West: Muslim missionary activity and the dynamics of conversion to Islam*. New York: Oxford University Press.

Prebish, C. S., & Baumann, M. (2002). *Westward Dharma: Buddhism beyond Asia*. Berkeley: University of California Press.

Rambo, L. R. (1993). *Understanding religious conversion*. New Haven: Yale University Press.

Röder, A. (2014). Explaining religious differences in immigrants' gender role attitudes: The changing impact of origin country and individual religiosity. *Ethnic and Racial Studies, 37*(14), 2615–2635.

Roos, L. (2010). Blod, rening och pånyttfödelse i judiska kvinnors liv. *Humanistportalen*. First published 2 June 2010. https://www.humanistportalen.se/artiklar/religionshistoria/?fbclid=IwAR3 lZYWkHyIL83jlFTj8ipPWoCynvCQkaSQ4EUPPe1MRG5mDjvoUP3rENcA

Roy, O. (2004). *Globalized Islam: The search for a new Ummah*. New York: Columbia University Press.

Rushdie, S. (1988). *The satanic verses*. London: Viking Penguin.

Sengupta, R., & Swamy, P. (2020). Hindutva in Europe: Making sense of diaspora contexts. In K. S. Jacobsen & F. Sardella (Eds.), *Handbook of Hinduism in Europe, volume 1*. Leiden: Brill.

Shah, S. (2018). *The making of a Gay Muslim: Religion, sexuality and identity in Malaysia and Britain*. London: Palgrave Macmillan.

Shannneik, Y. (2012). Conversion to Islam in Ireland: A Post-Catholic subjectivity? *Journal of Muslims in Europe, 1*(2), 166–188.

Soutar, L. (2010). British female converts to Islam: Choosing Islam as a rejection of individualism. *Language and Intercultural Communication, 10*(1), 3–16.

Stenberg, L. (1996). *Islamization of science: Four Muslim positions developing an Islamic modernity*. Stockholm: Almqvist & Wiksell International.

Stevanovic, N. (2012). *Remittances and moral economies of Bangladeshi New York immigrants in light of the economic crisis*. Online published PhD dissertation, Columbia University.

Sultán, M. (1999). Choosing Islam: A study of Swedish converts. *Social Compass, 46*(3), 325–335.

Thai, H. C. (2006). Money and masculinity among low wage Vietnamese immigrants in transnational families. *International Journal of Sociology of the Family, 32*(2), 247–271.

The Conversion Investigation. (2019). *Konvertutredningen. Rapport om Migrationsverkets hantering av konvertiters asylprocess*.

Thurfjell, D., & Willander, E. (2021). Muslims by ascription: On Post-Lutheran secularity and Muslim immigrants. *Numen, 68*(4), 307–335.

UNHCR. (2004). *Guidelines on international protection: Religion-based Refugee Claims under Article 1A(2) of the 1951 Convention and/or the 1967 Protocol relating to the Status of Refugees*. https://www.unhcr.org/uk/publications/legal/40d8427a4/guidelines-international-protection-6-religion-based-refugee-claims-under.html (Visited 19 July 2021).

Valentine, S. R. (2008). *Islam and the Ahmadiyya Jama'at: History, belief, practice*. New York: Columbia University Press.

Währisch-Oblau, C. (2009). *The missionary self-perception of Pentecostal/charismatic church leaders from the global South in Europe: Bringing Back the gospel*. Leiden: Brill.

Ward, K. (2006). *A history of global Anglicanism*. Cambridge: Cambridge University Press.

Werbner, P. (2003). *Pilgrims of love: The anthropology of a global Sufi cult*. London: Hurst & Company.

Wilson, H. F. (2017). On the paradox of "organized" encounters. *Journal of Intercultural Studies, 38*(6), 606–620.

Wohlrab-Sahr, M. (1999). *Konversion zum Islam in Deutschland und den USA*. Frankfurt/New York: Campus Verlag.

Zebiri, K. (2007). *British Muslim converts: Choosing alternative lives*. London: Oneworld Publications.

Open Access This chapter is licensed under the terms of the Creative Commons Attribution 4.0 International License (http://creativecommons.org/licenses/by/4.0/), which permits use, sharing, adaptation, distribution and reproduction in any medium or format, as long as you give appropriate credit to the original author(s) and the source, provide a link to the Creative Commons license and indicate if changes were made.

The images or other third party material in this chapter are included in the chapter's Creative Commons license, unless indicated otherwise in a credit line to the material. If material is not included in the chapter's Creative Commons license and your intended use is not permitted by statutory regulation or exceeds the permitted use, you will need to obtain permission directly from the copyright holder.

Chapter 6
Looking Ahead

In this final chapter, we venture to give some advice on researching religion and migration, first on what we know and then on what is lacking. If some readers heed our call and caution, it will be a needed and important contribution to far-too-neglected areas in migration research. By 'researchers' we mean students, scholars, journalists and others who seriously try to produce knowledge about the situation. Please feel included.

6.1 Bringing Religion into Migration Research

All through this book, we have tried to convey three key messages: (1) religion should not be overlooked in migration research designs as it is frequently very important to migrants; (2) the purposes for which religion is used and where expressions of it can be found cannot be regarded as fixed in any way; (3) religious norms and actual practices change over time and international migration is connected to these changes.

6.1.1 Religion in the Research Design of International Migration

It is an integral tradition in anthropology to pay attention to what the people you study consider important. Frequently, when reading the literature on migrants in Europe, we find that interviews contain references to features such as religious views, identities and rituals, without further analytical attention. Even if a researcher is not trained in the field, it is still pertinent to consider religious practices and ideas that informants claim are important. Fortunately, religious studies is not a mysterious field; a great deal of its theorisations are interlaced with those of contemporary sociology, anthropology and cultural studies.

In research on group identities, religious identifications cannot be reduced to a mere aspect of ethnicity, as this is simply not the case. Although religious identities and ethnicities frequently overlap, at times completely, the major religious identities – whether Catholic Church or Sunni Islam – are multi-ethnic. Statistically, Hinduism might primarily be the faith of people originating in India (but living in many corners of the globe), but India contains many ethnic groups (Kumar, 2004). Moreover, while group dynamics for ethnicities and religious identities might be very similar, the ethical, theological and ritual features of religions do not have equivalent parts in ethnicities. Finally, some ethnicities may harbour believers from different religions (Palestinian Arabs or Kurds for example) or, more commonly, different formulations of the same religion (see also Nordin, 2009; Baumann, 1999; Enloe, 1980).

Religious identities and ideas are potentially powerful, and can mobilise solidarity, friendship and even love for strangers – or the opposite. Failing to discover what religions mean to individuals or communities may allow international migration studies to miss a vital motivator in economic transactions, culture consumption, network analysis, political views, social engagement, gender roles, art production or even the very real act of migration itself.

Our recommendation is that migration researchers, in both qualitative and quantitative studies, try to include questions that identify the part played by religious perceptions and practices in the phenomena under investigation. When researching a group of people, talk to their religious leaders (and other community leaders), who can often explain a group's version of faith and contextualise what is happening within the group. Nonetheless, a word of caution: religious leaders tend to theologise the experience of believers and fix the relations between believer and faith (for example, claiming that a ritual act has a single specific function or meaning). From empirical studies, we know that both believers and non-believers approach religion in many ways, depending on socio-economic circumstances, individual experiences and life history.

6.1.2 The Function and Spaces of Religion

Be attentive to when and where religious belonging, identification and rituals have functions and are emphasised, and when not. Identities, ideas and interests are, for most people, situational (see discussion on moral registers in Chap. 3). Religious ideas, rituals, practices and behaviour can be identified even in outspoken atheists' lives and very worldly interests and passions can be found among the most pious people. In fact, expectations of clear divisions may hamper understanding. Religious emotions and ideas are immensely complex and can be triggered in the stoutest unbeliever by the beauty of nature, architecture, literature, music and solitude or accidents, sickness and grief. Most religious organisations catering to migrants are aware of this and will make use of aesthetics and nostalgia to provide a social context for the homesick, and counselling and help for the needy. Some do this efficiently, filling important functions in society – religious organisations are in general very decent, run by people who want to help others; however, there are those that are less benign whose primary interest lies in influence and money. What happens, and where, are tricky but important questions for research; in interviews, adherents tend to be loyal to the religious group they attend, at least initially.

During actual migration, religious space making is important for many migrants: a space to pray or meditate, alone or together with others. Journalists report on this in temporary camps like those along the French coast filled with migrants trying to cross to the UK. The efforts put into this space making suggests that the migrants consider this crucial, but for what? Their wellbeing, spiritual needs, hopes or anxieties? Researchers need to try to work in these difficult areas to explore the function and spaces of religions during migration.

6.1.3 Changing Religious Norms and Actual Practices

Researchers need to be aware of the difference between written or verbalised norms, on the one hand, and actual practices on the other. Lived religiosity is context sensitive; functions and expressions cannot be taken for granted. Still, some things are surprisingly resilient over time.

When researching migrants and paying attention to the role religion(s) play in their life and their migration experience, textbooks on religions may be helpful. Yet textbooks can only do so much if they are attempting to cover hundreds or thousands of years of development. Further, most religions have minority groups that are not even addressed in an introductory textbook. There will likely be special volumes on these too but, again, the coverage must be understood in relation to the limitations of the form.

An example: prayer practices are interesting in relation to migrants' religion and we need to understand them in context. We may learn a lot about prayer from a textbook or by asking a religious leader; it may add to the knowledge needed to understand the discursive relations between the studied migrants and prayer. In interviews about personal religious practices, religious interviewees often relate religious norms in attempts to meet expectations, while in their private lives they must create themselves as individuals in light of their knowledge of the norms, their personal practices and possible discrepancies. When in migration, how and why do relations with prayer – knowledge of the norms and actual practices – change over time or remain static? These are tricky things to explore. Researchers need to be careful and attentive to avoid reducing prayers to simple questions about practice and regularity.

Historicise, contextualise and see relations with religious identities, discourses and practices as exactly that: relations that must be upheld and negotiated, that can change and morph into something else while retaining names, symbols or rituals. At times, observed religious communities, rituals or beliefs, as yet unnamed, defy established practices and conceptualisations. New interpretations, new configurations and even new religions may appear in new settings when social conditions change. Charismatic leaders tend to appear at such times and US history, in particular, is full of such instances.

6.2 What We Do Not Know

This section addresses blank areas in our knowledge of religion and migration. Clearly, we have been selective; however, we consider the following areas crucial, as research on them is very scarce indeed (we have already mentioned some areas in Chap. 5). We begin with historical research and then move on to contemporary phenomena. We have striven to make this section forward looking with the intent to stimulate research we would like to see done in future.

6.2.1 Historical Perspectives

Most migration research concerned with religion focuses on synchronic perspectives, possibly with a history of the group concerned as an informative backdrop. What is needed are projects following populations over time as some migration research of the labour market has succeeded in doing. All the questions we have raised above – from religious change over time and generation to different stages of the migrationship process – are possible to pose to a well-crafted research project examining long-term processes. Particularly interesting is religious change over time in individual lives.

Typically, in religious environments, religious socialisation takes place in childhood and young people subsequently tend to strive to sort out, confirm, engage in or reject the religious heritage. Young adults generally are allowed flexibility in relation to religion, not least if they are engaged in higher studies. Later, work and family life often restrict the time spent on religious engagement. However, in old age, religion may return.

Is this admittedly sketchy version of European religious trajectories true for immigrants whose old country ways must be considered? While researchers have engaged with the religious development of immigrant children, youth and young adults, far fewer have addressed the religious attachment and thoughts of older immigrants. In a way this is puzzling as one reason to focus on young adults is their accessibility as informants, yet many older retired immigrants will likely also have time on their hands and can easily be reached through religious organisations or cultural clubs. Classical ethnographic life-story interviews supported by letters, diaries and photo albums would likely be a good start.

Another side of historical research is engaging with the period specifically not mentioned in this book: religious migration to Europe before WWII. Some remarkable research on the European colonial powers, slaves, businesspeople and intellectuals has already been done (e.g., Asmay, 2021; Sorgenfrei, 2018; Offermanns, 2003), but much more is needed. To detail lives through archival research is fascinating and stimulating work although the ideal material rarely surfaces; rather, names turn up once in a newspaper, a police report, a departmental dispatch or on a tombstone and then no more. But at times reports, diaries and newspaper clippings can be puzzled together, most easily for successful migrants. The accessibility of computerised archives and newspapers makes it possible to attempt the research even if writing an undergraduate or MA dissertation.

6.2.2 *Developing More Reliable Statistics*

As mentioned in Chap. 1, while data on age, assumed sex, nationality and certain information on economic issues such as employment can be provided by states, NGOs or the EU, researchers scavenging for good data on such basics as nominal religious affiliation are generally disappointed. At times states have legal barriers to gathering such information while the EU's General Data Protection Regulation considers religious belonging sensitive personal data. Often, any data on religious belonging will have to be gathered by researchers rather than drawn from registers.

Assumptions may be made from register data: for example, citizenship (even former) can be drawn from such sources and it may be assumed on this basis that if Turkey is a country with a 99.8 percent Muslim population (as the government claims), the same percentage of Turkish migrants to Europe are Muslims. Still, despite being a very minor group (far less than 1% of the Turkish population), we know that a disproportionately large number of Christian Turks have migrated to Sweden, accounting for maybe a third of Turkish immigrants – at least before the mid-1990s (Sander, 1993). Further, Muslim belonging is a diverse category. In Turkey the majority are Hanafi Sunni Muslims, but the Alevi are a large minority that some Alevis consider Shia, others see as separate from both Sunni and Shia and yet others as primarily a cultural rather than religious tradition. Estimates of the number of Alevis in Turkey range from 10 to 33 percent, making it hard to operate with assumptions (Cagaptay, 2014: 83). Twelver Shia Muslims also make up approximately 4 percent of the population while Sunni Muslims are split between government-loyal Hanafi Sunnis and a plethora of other Sunni groups like Süleymanlı, Hizmet and Milli Görüş.

This is but one example, but religious statistics tend to be absent, primitive, flawed or all three, both in countries of origin and in Europe – particularly statistics on actual religious practices and beliefs. The existing data and statistical studies on Muslims in Europe have been reviewed and harshly criticised as shallow and built on uniformising categories (Johansen & Spielhaus, 2012). What is needed is quantitative data built on large surveys, preferably designed by professional statisticians trained in multivariate analysis collaborating with migration theory-conscious humanists or social scientists with an in-depth knowledge of the tricky variable 'religion'. However, such studies have proved very difficult to conduct and large surveys are quite expensive. Some general quantitative studies of sampled populations, like the World Values Survey,[1] or whole populations, like the UK Office of National Statistics survey,[2] have been conducted, but these are not geared to the specific interests of religion and migration studies.

6.2.3 Comparative Perspectives

To be able to formulate valid theories, researchers need to investigate numerous cases, preferably involving various religious traditions in different countries. Some brave synthesis has been attempted, (e.g., Kivisto, 2014; Ebaugh, 2010; Warner, 2000), but more needs to be done, taking more variables into account. Big data holds a certain promise for both qualitative analysis inspired by intersectional analysis and quantitative, multivariate analysis. This requires experts in different fields to join forces, which is what is happening in some large-scale, digital humanities projects. To be able to address the *longue durée* comparatively, a group of researchers would have to be granted funding for a large-scale project covering years of research like some of the most ambitious US-based projects mentioned in Chap. 2. Such projects could be game-changers for the field. In most cases, comparisons must be made in relation to previous research and again it is important to ferret out fine studies from different countries, despite language barriers.

6.2.4 The Role of Social Media for Religion in Relation to Migration

As mentioned, social media connects people in ways hard to imagine some decades ago. Today, everything from crucial religious rituals to family events can be followed anywhere with a digital connection. Thirty years ago, the birth of a child to immigrant parents would be announced to relatives in the homeland with a letter and photograph or an expensive telephone call; nowadays grandparents can initiate online relations with a grandchild immediately after delivery. As group attachment and socialisation are important factors in the development of religion – as is the transition from being childless to having children – researchers need to investigate whether social media has a role for migrants in upholding, developing and changing religion (e.g., Ferguson et al., 2021; Trysnes & Synnes, 2022).

---

[1] https://www.worldvaluessurvey.org/wvs.jsp

[2] https://www.ons.gov.uk/peoplepopulationandcommunity/culturalidentity/religion

6.2 What We Do Not Know

Such research faces several challenges as even delineating the field requires input from informants. Further, researchers will have to collaborate closely with migrants and be allowed to follow their social media activities, documenting informants' activities using the latest technology. Such research raises ethical complexities requiring attention before research starts and also as they appear. At times, researchers will need to compartmentalise to be able to frame the field, despite knowing that one or two media channels are only part of the full media flow.

Research on media and rituals could be developed for social media, migration and religion questions. For example, Ronald Grimes (2002) suggests looking at ritual action in virtual spaces including playful (ludic) rituals in games, mediatised rituals including marriages conducted with the partners in different places, and interactive, mediatised sacred objects and texts, just to mention a few things of interest. Can this be combined with migration research? Researchers need to find ways to adjust the very active social media research field to accommodate religion and migration. The 2020–22 pandemic saw some research on religious rituals that have moved online due to physical distancing rules (see Grafton, 2021) and it is likely that any successful mediatisation will become part of future standard repertoires. If a devotee migrant misses the weekly sermons of a charismatic leader of choice due to migrating to another country, for instance, they may now participate in (or at least follow) them online, in real time.

Finally, as religious celebrities, authorities, monks, rabbis and imams take to TikTok, Instagram and Twitter, their accounts have become among the most popular in the world, raising issues about how religious authority can be analysed. Is there an ongoing transformation whereby the authority of traditional religious offices is being complemented by other – more personal (or humanising?) – elements, like the singing, dancing, joking, pranking or baking religious leader? Is this especially important in a minority position where religious authority is less institutionalised and more personalised (or charismatic if turning to Weber's terminology)?

6.2.5 Lingering Immigrant Identities

An intriguing, partly disturbing phenomenon is the lingering identification as 'migrant', 'immigrant' or even 'foreigner', both by the established and the newcomers and their children. It is not surprising that ethnic consciousness is retained in families and by outsiders; that is to be expected, especially given modern communication technologies. Nor is it surprising that families remember and at times celebrate their migration history (or complex of histories). The phenomenon that needs attention is why members of the second generation are still identified by others and at times by themselves as immigrants. This is likely due to a mix of immigration politics, class, economic position and discourses on 'race' (not least racialised othering where whiteness is a key category), ethnic identification, national identity and religion. Different country-based, regional or local cases should be compared to theorise this properly: on a micro level among individuals; on a meso level – both in-group and out-group; and on a macro level, taking into consideration state politics and policies. Again, longer perspectives would benefit conclusions drawn.

Researchers should also be open to ongoing terminological reinterpretations, as immigrants (or equivalent) may encourage group empowerment by appropriating terminology that is meant to exclude. A similar development is taking place with racist slurs, with some of the terminological reinterpretations involving religious identities. It would be rewarding to develop theories concerning the role of religion in all this. For example, religious belonging clearly plays a role in anti-immigrant political propaganda all over Europe and those responsible for it have a vested interest in confining people to categories of otherness, shunning hybridity and fluid identifications; equating the religious other with the immigrant thus becomes a trope. In this, we sense an opportunity to combine the strong research on the Jewish other, Islamophobia and racism with, for example, migration research on political discourse and the economy.

6.2.6 Religious Change in Society in General and Among Established Religious Communities

Does migration change attitudes to religious rituals, ideas and belonging among the established? In a globalising world interconnected by a myriad of media channels and technologies, isolating one cause for possible change is risky. Nonetheless, if the newly arrived in a given European country not only practice other religions but also demonstrate different attitudes to religious rituals, morals, ethics and belonging, and if the established live and/or work alongside them, it is fair to ask if this affects attitudes and behaviour among the latter. Comparisons between cities and areas in cities should be possible, at least on a surface level. Are there changes in the wearing of visible religious symbols, attendance at rituals or even engagement in activities? Are there differences if people belong to an established majority or an established minority? Are immigrants of the same overall religion as the established more or less likely to trigger change among the established than if they engage in other religions? Are youth more or less likely to be affected? Is there a difference in shallow contacts and profound ones? Most projects have focused on the reverse, on how the religions of the migrants are affected, but as the ideological discourse on integration stipulates: integration is not a one-sided process.

For example, a study on how the Church of Sweden meets new challenges generated by migration discloses many interesting aspects worthy of further research. The study discusses whether the Church – still by far the largest religious denomination in the country – should only take responsibility for its own members or should also assume responsibility for members of other congregations and for irregular migrants who are not being recognised as citizens in the country – a responsibility it had when it was the state church. One conclusion is that basic values must be reflected upon and negotiated. What values can the Church of Sweden not give up? What can it learn and include from immigrant churches to become a church that is relevant to all Swedes, immigrants as well as non-immigrants (Helgesson Kjellin, 2016)? The Church of Sweden still organises more than half the population but is very aware of the changing religious atmosphere in the country. We are likely to find changes relating to migration on many levels.

We also need to investigate changes in religion among majority populations by looking beyond national or state borders and trying to capture transnational flows. We know, for example, that rituals change: some become fashionable before disappearing, some become more permanent features. Can this be connected to migration or is it more likely connected to the globalisation of ideas?

6.3 Final Words

This book has had the overall aim to inform, inspire and challenge. Religious rituals, ideas and belongings – the three main fields in religious studies – have played roles in migration throughout human history and continue to do so. When researching migration issues, this should not be forgotten in research designs. These fields are not neatly compartmentalised and separated from contemporary society in Europe; on the contrary, states regulate religious expression and belonging, assigning different rights to different groups, and the established and newcomers alike have specific relations with religious rituals, ideas and belongings which affect how they go about their everyday business and perceive the world. Neither are religious convictions distinct from the economy, politics or the labour market. Migration researchers need not add the broad examination of religion to every project but, given that migration theories largely ignore religion, we suggest researchers at least consider it as a possible complexity in the fields they study.

References

Asmay, Y. S. (2021). *Islam in Victorian Liverpool: An Ottoman account of Britain's first mosque community*. Swansea: Claritas.

Baumann, G. (1999). *The multicultural riddle: Rethinking national, ethnic and religious identities*. London: Routledge.

Cagaptay, S. (2014). *The rise of Turkey: The twenty-first century's first Muslim power*. Sterling, VA: Potomac Books.

Ebaugh, H. R. (2010). Transnationality and religion in immigrant congregations: The global impact. *Nordic Journal of Religion and Society, 23*(2), 105–119.

Enloe, C. (1980). Religion and ethnicity. In P. F. Sugar (Ed.), *Ethnic diversity and conflict in Eastern Europe* (pp. 350–360). Santa Barbara: ABC-Clio.

Ferguson, J., Ecklund, E. H., & Rothschild, C. (2021). Navigating religion online: Jewish and Muslim responses to social media. *Religions, 12*(4), 258. https://doi.org/10.3390/rel12040258

Grafton, D. D. (Ed.). (2021). Muslim-Christian Relations in the Midst of the COVID-19 Pandemic, special issue. *The Muslim World, 111*(4), 563–572.

Grimes, R. L. (2002). Ritual and the media. In S. M. Hoover & L. Schofield Clark (Eds.), *Practicing religion in the age of the media*. New York: Columbia University Press.

Helgesson Kjellin, K. (2016). *En bra plats att vara på: En antropologisk studie av mångfaldsarbete och identitetsskapande inom Svenska kyrkan*. Skellefteå: Artos.

Johansen, B. S., & Spielhaus, R. (2012). Counting deviance: Revisiting a decade's production of surveys among Muslims in Western Europe. *Journal of Muslims in Europe, 1*(1), 81–112.

Kivisto, P. (2014). *Religion and immigration: Migrant faiths in North America and Western Europe*. Malden, MA: Polity.

Kumar, P. P. (2004). Taxonomy of the Indian diaspora in South Africa: Problems and issues in defining their identity. In K. A. Jacobsen (Ed.), *South Asians in the diaspora: Histories and religious traditions* (pp. 375–392). Leiden: Leiden.

Nordin, M. (2009). Religion och etnicitet. In A. Bremborg-Davidsson, G. Gustafsson, & G. Hallonsten (Eds.), *Religionssociologi i brytningstider* (Lund studies in sociology of religion) (pp. 284–297). Lund: Lund University.

Offermanns, J. (2003). *Der lange Weg des Zen-Buddhismus nach Deutschland. Vom 16. Jahrhundert bis Rudolf Otto*. Lund: Lund University.

Sander, Å. (1993). *I vilken utsträckning är den svenska muslimen religiös?* Centrum för studier av kulturkontakt och internationell migration, Göteborgs universitet.

Sorgenfrei, S. (2018). *Islam i Sverige: De första 1300 åren*. Stockholm: Myndigheten för stöd till trossamfund.

Trysnes, I., & Synnes, R. M. (2022). 'The role of religion in young Muslims' and Christians' self-presentation on social media. *Young, 30*(3), 281–296.

Warner, S. (2000). Religion and new (Post-1965) immigrants: Some principles drawn from field research. *American Studies, 41*(2), 267–286.

Open Access This chapter is licensed under the terms of the Creative Commons Attribution 4.0 International License (http://creativecommons.org/licenses/by/4.0/), which permits use, sharing, adaptation, distribution and reproduction in any medium or format, as long as you give appropriate credit to the original author(s) and the source, provide a link to the Creative Commons license and indicate if changes were made.

The images or other third party material in this chapter are included in the chapter's Creative Commons license, unless indicated otherwise in a credit line to the material. If material is not included in the chapter's Creative Commons license and your intended use is not permitted by statutory regulation or exceeds the permitted use, you will need to obtain permission directly from the copyright holder.

If you have any concerns about our products,
you can contact us on
ProductSafety@springernature.com

In case Publisher is established outside the EU,
the EU authorized representative is:
**Springer Nature Customer Service Center GmbH
Europaplatz 3, 69115 Heidelberg, Germany**

Printed by Libri Plureos GmbH
in Hamburg, Germany